"A refreshingly grace-filled and intelligent discussion on the ever-daunting topic of sex. . . . Read this book, share it with friends and pass it around. Not only will you find things your mother never told you, you will find things society, church and culture never told you. These pages contain a no-nonsense honesty that, if applied, will change our lives and the lives of those we seek to love."

Shayne Moore, author of *Refuse to Do Nothing*

"Redemptive, wise, practical, honest and tender, this book is a welcome addition to the conversation about women's sexuality."

Sarah Bessey, author of *Jesus Feminist*

"Kim Eckert deepens the discussion about sex to a profound exploration of our sexual soul. Practical and redemptive, this book explores who you are as a woman intimately connected to a loving God, to yourself and to others. Truly a provocative, fabulous read!"

Marnie C. Ferree, LMFT, CSAT, author of *No Stones: Women Redeemed from Sexual Addiction*

"Kim Gaines Eckert gives Christian women a much needed sexual voice. She thoughtfully dispels distorting sexual myths, brings wisdom to cultural pressures and gets to the heart of female concerns. This book conveys hope and redemption within a sexually confusing world. It is an excellent read for men as well as women."

Doug Rosenau, author of *A Celebration of Sex*

THINGS YOUR MOTHER NEVER TOLD YOU

A Woman's Guide to Sexuality

KIM GAINES ECKERT

IVP Books

An imprint of InterVarsity Press
Downers Grove, Illinois

InterVarsity Press
P.O. Box 1400, Downers Grove, IL 60515-1426
World Wide Web: www.ivpress.com
Email: email@ivpress.com

InterVarsity Press® is the book-publishing division of InterVarsity Christian Fellowship/USA®, a movement of students and faculty active on campus at hundreds of universities, colleges and schools of nursing in the United States of America, and a member movement of the International Fellowship of Evangelical Students. For information about local and regional activities, write Public Relations Dept., InterVarsity Christian Fellowship/USA, 6400 Schroeder Rd., P.O. Box 7895, Madison, WI 53707-7895, or visit the IVCF website at www.intervarsity.org.

All Scripture quotations, unless otherwise indicated, are taken from THE HOLY BIBLE, NEW INTERNATIONAL VERSION®, NIV® Copyright © 1973, 1978, 1984, 2011 by Biblica, Inc.™ Used by permission. All rights reserved worldwide.

While all stories in this book are true, some names and identifying information in this book have been changed to protect the privacy of the individuals involved.

Cover design: Cindy Kiple
Interior design: Beth Hagenberg

Images: woman's face: © Mohamad Itani/Trevillion Images;
   torn brown paper: © GaryAlvis/iStockphoto;
   vintage frame: © aleksandar velasevic/iStockphoto

ISBN 978-0-8308-4309-1 (print)
ISBN 978-0-8308-7187-2 (digital)

Printed in the United States of America ∞

Library of Congress Cataloging-in-Publication Data

Eckert, Kim Gaines, 1974-
   Things your mother never told you / Kim Gaines Eckert.
      pages cm
   Includes bibliographical references.
   ISBN 978-0-8308-4309-1 (pbk. : alk. paper)
   1. Sex--Religious aspects--Christianity. 2. Christian women—Sexual behavior. I. Title.
   BT708.E25 2013
   241'.664--dc23

                                                          2013044245

P   18   17   16   15   14   13   12   11   10   9   8   7   6   5   4   3   2   1
Y   29   28   27   26   25   24   23   22   21   20   19   18   17   16   15   14

For Jeff,

my partner on the journey in every way

Contents

1 You Are Sexual and It Is Good   9

2 More Than an Act   19

3 Beyond the Battle of the Sexes   34

4 Sexual Self-Image in a Girls-Gone-Wild World   51

5 The Shame of Silence   69

6 Sex, Power and *Fifty Shades of Grey*   82

7 Healing from Unwanted Sexual Experiences   94

8 Sexual Disappointment   106

9 Redemptive Sexuality   122

Appendix A: Going Deeper   137
    A Guide for Growth and Reflection

Appendix B: Growing in Community   153
    A Group Discussion Guide

Further Reading   158

Acknowledgments   161

Notes   163

1

You Are Sexual and It Is Good

The dream of finding our end,
the thing we were made for, in a Heaven
of purely human love could not be true
unless our whole Faith were wrong.
We were made for God.

C. S. Lewis,
The Four Loves

The Colorado summer night air breezed around my face, and as we walked I could feel my breath catch every few minutes when his hand would accidentally (or not) brush my arm or my hand. We talked with the intensity of youth and romance and idealism about everything we could think of—our families and friends, our dreams and futures. But even with all the talking, I was constantly aware of the freshly washed scent of his hair, the feel of his breath on my cheek when he turned and laughed at something I said, and how my stomach turned a bit when he gave me a certain look. As we stepped onto the walking bridge and he slid his hand into mine, I could hardly hear him talking at all. I was seventeen years old, and I was falling in love for the first time.

I had been preparing to fall in love for much of my young life. As a daddy's girl and the youngest sister of three older brothers, I grew up with my fair share of male attention at home. I made my dad read *Cinderella* to me so many times that the book's binding fell apart. All the fairy tales of my childhood told me that happiness comes when Prince Charming arrives and saves me with a kiss.

As an adolescent, I did plenty of dating. Most of the boys I went out with, however, were less than the Prince Charming of my fantasies. But on that magical, summer night, my fantasies about falling in love began to come true. As we sat at the end of the walking bridge and he leaned over to kiss me for the first time, I just knew this was it—*he* was it. This was what I had been waiting for my whole life. As a seventeen-year-old girl, I bought into one of many myths surrounding romance and sexuality: that it would make me happy and complete.

Why was I so drawn to that particular young man that summer? Some would suggest one short and sweet answer to the question: sex! We were sexually attracted to each other, which affected our bodies, emotions and thoughts in particular ways. Although it may seem crass to focus on sexuality as a primary motivator for innocent, young love, we will miss a huge piece of the picture if we ignore it. Freud called sexuality one of the two driving or motivating forces in human life, and although our puritanical Christian tradition might lead us to want to disagree with Freud in all things, his observation of human nature in this respect is actually quite accurate.

Sexual feelings and desires lead us to act in strange and surprising ways. Emboldened by the magic of love, we will say embarrassing things and act out dramatic, romantic gestures. We leave jobs and move miles away from our families to be with our beloved. We do not do these things because of sex in the simplest sense of the term (as a physical act between two people). Rather, we do these things because we are sexual beings who have been created with a longing for love, connection and intimacy. Sexuality is the very thing that creates that deep longing. God created us in his image, as sexual beings, and sexuality creates a deep desire in us for union with another—physical and otherwise—to be joined or made one with someone outside ourselves.

MYTH: SEX IS GOD OR SEX IS EVIL

Many years ago, Freud described sex as a motivator for human behavior, and for anyone who has ever turned on a television, walked past a row of magazines in a store, or seen movie posters or previews, it is obvious that many people agree with him. Movies and TV shows are filled with explicit sexual conversations, provocatively dressed characters and sultry sex scenes. Even many children's TV shows and movies contain sexual innuendos. Magazines are filled with advice on how to attract members of the opposite sex, how to have more sex, how to try new sexual positions or how to achieve better orgasms. Clearly, sexual material gets our attention, and our popular culture supports and spreads one of many myths around sexuality—that sex is a god.

At the outset, though, I do want to say that sex is a gift, and it is good! Our identity as sexual beings, created male or female in God's image, leads us to a deep longing for intimacy and connection with others who are different from us. This, too, is a good gift! Sometimes, however, sex is no longer seen as a gift created by God for our good, but it is seen as a god to be worshiped and pursued in its own right. We have begun worshiping the creation, sex, rather than the Creator, God (Romans 1:25).

Philip Yancey puts it this way, "Sex no longer points to something beyond; it becomes the thing itself, the substitute sacred."[1] Because sexuality can be so powerful and pleasurable, we may be tempted to confuse the gift with the giver. But neither our identity as sexual beings, nor the gift of sexual pleasure, is the thing itself. God has created us for union with himself, and sex and sexuality are signs that point us toward that ultimate good. Sex *is* wonderful, but it is not the ultimate. When we mistake it for such, we are bound to be disappointed.

While much of our popular culture supports the myth that sex is a god, others take the opposite approach, viewing sexuality with suspicion or even disdain. In response to how sexuality has been perverted and distorted, some people appear to view sex as something that is, in itself, broken. Instead of idealizing or worshiping it, sexuality itself is demonized. Our Christian subculture can, at times, directly or tacitly play into another damaging myth—that sex is evil.

As a teenager falling in love for the first time, I was influenced by both these idealizing and demonizing myths surrounding sexuality. On the surface, it may not have looked like I was following the "sex is a god" myth; after all, I wasn't actually *having* sex. I did, however, fall into the trap of believing that the relationship was the one thing that was going to make me complete and happy.

The lessons of fairy-tale romances were not the only messages I had received about sexuality, though, which led to feelings of confusion and guilt about how I felt around my boyfriend. Some of the other lessons I received in church or youth group told me, in seemingly a hundred different ways, that sex before marriage is bad. It often felt like a few of those words were louder than the others, as in, "SEX (before marriage) IS BAD!" I know my youth group and church leaders wanted to protect us, as teenagers, from the damage that can come from making poor sexual choices, as some of the leaders who were most passionate about this message openly acknowledged their own shame and regret about sexual choices in their past. However, despite their good intentions these messages left me feeling guilty for even *having* sexual feelings toward my boyfriend, much less acting on them.

For many women, the myth that sex is evil and the resulting feelings of confusion and shame persist even after entering into marriage, because we have focused on all the ways to *not* indulge sexual feelings for so many years. The wedding ceremony is supposed to magically flip the switch so that now those feelings can be fully engaged in and lead to euphoric and guilt-free sex: something that has been off-limits or bad for so long "should" suddenly feel like a beautiful, God-given expression of love and commitment. However, I have counseled many women who experienced a deep sense of disappointment and guilt about their inability to enjoy sex as a gift in marriage. Even though they *know* that sex within marriage is not a sin; it still *feels* like a sin.

In and of themselves, abstinence campaigns and messages like "true love waits" are not bad, and they are certainly not the only way we pick up ideas about sexuality. In fact, we also learn about sexuality through what is *not* talked about in our homes and churches. The silence that surrounds sexuality is often experienced as shameful because, if we can't talk about something, it is easy to conclude it must be bad.

For others, sex feels evil because of how it has been used or misused. A vast number of women have experienced some kind of unwanted sexual experience or sexual abuse. Despite head knowledge about what sex is meant to be, the pain and hurt these women have experienced leaves an emotional scar. When our sexuality has been violated, it can be hard to reconcile our own experiences with what sex is *intended* to be as a reflection of God's love and character. Consequently, sex itself may be viewed with fear and anger.

But, sexuality is not evil, nor is it a god. When we buy into either of these myths, we move away from the truth of what sexuality is in God's creative design. While sexuality in our culture is often depicted in ways that are disconnecting or even degrading, it was actually designed to ultimately lead us away from a selfish focus on our needs and wants into a desire to give and share with another—to share our bodies, our hearts and our lives. Throughout this book, I will examine myths like the two in this section so we can see how they keep us from experiencing sexual wholeness.

A VISION FOR SEXUAL WHOLENESS

As a psychologist, women often come to me for help in their journeys toward healing and wholeness. An honest conversation with a client about her longing to become whole, however, is ultimately going to be grounded in what it means for her to become a whole *woman*. Because sexuality is core to our personhood, to become a whole woman is to become sexually whole as well.

Conversations about sex and sexuality matter, because they are really conversations about personhood and identity. When we hear the word *sex*, we often associate that with either sexual intercourse *or* with gender assignment (male or female). Although sexuality includes both of those, it encompasses so much more. Our identity as sexual beings is why we are drawn to give ourselves to another person both physically and emotionally. It is why my teenage heart skipped a beat when my boyfriend entered the room, and it is why I relish time alone with my husband today. It is not just a physical urge designed to keep the species going; rather, this is how God created us in his image—as gendered, sexual beings with deep longings for union with another.

Becoming sexually whole means that we learn to listen to our sexuality, trusting it as a good that God has created. We can listen to our sexuality by learning the important lessons it offers about God, about ourselves and about the life that God is calling us to *now*—in addition to seeing the vision of the life he has created us for, one of constant love and physical union with him in eternity.

Our sexuality is who we are as women. It is not just a *part* of us, like our breasts or our vaginas are, and it is not merely our bodies, just the flesh to be conquered. Nor is it only for *some* of us, like the "sexy" ones; rather, sexuality is intrinsic to all of us. We need to stop listening to compartmentalizing and dehumanizing messages about sexuality in general and female sexuality in particular. Authentic sexuality should always make us more human, not less so. Sexuality should be connecting, not disconnecting. Sexuality is part and parcel of our whole selves; it is not just one part of us. We are ensouled bodies and embodied souls, and our sexuality matters.

Sexuality is also intricately tied up with how we live. Because we are made in God's image, we reflect his character and personhood in our lives. Our sexuality is central to our identity, and so it matters what we do with our bodies and how we live out our sexuality. The practical choices my high school boyfriend and I made about what to do and not do sexually impacted our relationship, and they also affected the extent to which our relationship was able to accurately reflect God's nature. As Christians, our task is not just to ask ethical or moral questions about sexual behavior, but to ask what it means to be human, sexual, gendered beings in light of God's character and purpose for sexuality, which will be explored throughout this book.[2]

Grace. Before we begin this journey of examining what it means to be and live as sexual creatures made in God's image, I would like to offer a theme word to hang onto in the following chapters: *grace.* If you find yourself feeling confused or frustrated or even overwhelmed as you read and think about what it means to be and live as a sexual being, I would encourage you to return to that simple word as a guidepost for our journey together.

Sex and sexuality are complex. They are not easy topics with simple answers. Although it is tempting to reduce the questions to black-and-white answers, we must instead examine sexuality with grace-filled eyes. In our churches and culture, we are offered many oversimplified messages: *You are either a virgin or you're not. You are either exclusively homosexual or you're exclusively heterosexual. Sexual addiction and lust are men's issues only.* We are surrounded by reductionistic messages about sex that are often simply untrue. As we embark on this journey, let me challenge you to refuse to accept simplistic answers.

The mystery of sexuality requires that we approach questions with humility, and that we journey toward sexual wholeness in and through the grace of God. When we freely acknowledge that we do not have all the answers, we can intentionally fight against the black-and-white simplicities our culture and even our churches sometimes offer about sex.

As Christians, we are called to be countercultural, and we can and should see, think and live out our sexuality differently. A grace-oriented approach means respecting and embracing its mystery. The way we experience our sexuality is mysterious—whether we are married or single, young or old—so we can stop trying to find a simple answer for how to live it out. Rather we can live in the questions and the beauty of that mystery, trusting that God is using our sexual identity and experiences to point us toward the thing itself: ultimate union with Christ.

HOW TO READ THIS BOOK

This book is intended to help you develop a healthy, whole and uniquely female sexuality. To do so, we will explore what it means to have an integrated sexuality—to see and accept our sexuality as a created good, and to incorporate the feelings and longings sexuality brings into our personhood, instead of denying, rejecting, misusing or overfocusing on particular aspects of our sexuality.

Throughout this book, I will focus on pervasive, damaging myths about sexuality that can keep us from experiencing sexual wholeness. From "sex is just an act" to "what you have done (or had done to you) is who you are," we will investigate how these myths affect us, as well as how we can experience Christ's redemption in our sexuality.

We will study both who we *are* as fundamentally relational, sexual, gendered beings, as well as how we are called to reflect that loving, relational nature in the way we *live* our sexual, gendered lives. Theological foundations for our sexual identity and the relationship between sex and gender will be evaluated.

We will survey how we learn about sexuality, both through overt cultural messages and shameful silences. We will look at the rela-

tionship between sex and power, and how that plays out in phenomena like sex scandals and the erotic bestseller *Fifty Shades of
Grey*. Ways to grow and heal from sexual wounds and disappointment
will also be examined. Finally, I will open up ways to live out sexual
redemption in community with others.

Sexual restoration is one part of the whole drama of God restoring
humanity and creation to himself. Therefore, part of what we are
called to do is not just move toward healing and growth in our own
lives but also look for ways to move others toward healing and growth.

My hope is that this book will assist you on your path toward
healing and wholeness in your sexual identity, but I hope you will not
stop there. God grows us up and transforms us not only for ourselves
but also for others. Therefore, I will explore ways we can use our own
healing to participate in God's full story of sexual restoration and redemption—for a sexually whole community. One tangible way to
begin the process of participating in God's full story of sexual restoration and redemption is to read this book in community. I would
encourage you to seek out a trusted friend, counselor or small group
to read this book with you. Healing and growth happen in the context
of relationship. We can learn, grow and be challenged exponentially
by reflecting on and sharing our stories with others, as well as listening to and learning from others' stories.

In appendix B, you will find a group study guide. The discussion
questions are designed to guide conversations about who you are as
a sexual being, and how you can live out that reality in a way that
reflects God's loving nature to a broken world. In appendix A, you
will find an in-depth guide for growth and reflection called "Going
Deeper." Here you will be prompted to engage in guided journaling
activities and offered interventions to try that I use with my own
counseling clients.

Whether you are reading this book with others or alone, I highly
recommend finding a quiet space with your journal and a cup of

coffee to dig into the "Going Deeper" appendix. For something to have lasting impact, we have to engage in an *active* learning process. When you reflect on and actually write out responses to sentence prompts, when you engage in quieting visualizations, or when you draw your model of sexuality and gender, these activities allow you to move from the position of a passive recipient to an active participant in the text.

Whether you read this book in a small group, with a trusted friend or on your own, my prayer is that God will use these words as an instrument of healing and redemption in your own life and in the lives of others.

2

More Than an Act

God not only made our bodies
but equipped them with hormones,
a nervous system, physical sensations,
thought patterns and a psychological
capacity to help us find connection
with others. It seems we were
made for each other!

Jack and Judith Balswick,
Authentic Human Sexuality

After getting my kids to bed and collapsing onto the couch last
week, I grabbed the remote to wind down after a long day of managing sibling tiffs and power struggles. A familiar sitcom with sexually charged banter and dialogue flashed onto the screen. A man
in his twenties, speaking to a buddy about a mutual female friend,
stated confidently, "I'd do her!" This phrase gave me pause. How
many times, unfortunately, have I heard men and women alike
reduce God's gift of sexual union to a mere behavioral release,
such as "doing *it*," or the even more dehumanizing phrases, "doing
her" or "doing *him*"?

Furthermore, I have noticed a new use of the term *sexy* lately. Instead of this word being relegated to descriptions of men and women who are dressed or behaving in particularly erotic ways, it is being applied to a wide range of activities or objects. Ariel Levy notes this pattern in her book *Female Chauvinist Pigs*, where she challenges ways that women have internalized our culture's hypersexualization: "For something to be noteworthy it must be 'sexy,'" Levy writes. "Sexiness is no longer just about being arousing or alluring, it's about being worthwhile."[1]

As examples, I have heard church pastors apologize that their church activities are "not very sexy"; I have listened to academics discuss certain research topics as more "sexy" than others; and I have overheard techies talking about how one computer operating system is "sexier" than another operating system. I sometimes wonder when the word *sexy* got coopted by the general public to mean something that has seemingly little to do with sex. This has broad implications for how we think and feel about sex. If sexy equals something that is valuable or worthwhile, then sex equals value or worth. What does it mean for us if we equate the value and worth of objects, people and activities with their "sex appeal"?

Sex sells in American culture, and like all American women, I am assaulted on a daily basis by physical or verbal depictions of women in subservient physical and sexual positions. And just like the sitcom I stumbled on, degrading images of female sexuality are everywhere — in movies, on the Internet, at the shopping mall, on magazine covers at the grocery store with my kids, or walking around town with my husband. The dehumanizing language and images that we are surrounded by teach important things about sexuality in general and female sexuality in particular.

Too often in our culture, sex is depicted through language and imagery that has little to do with beauty, love and intimacy. Rather, sex is presented as a depersonalized and even desexualized act of self-pleasure, involving some other person or even thing. Sexuality becomes simply appetite, friction, desire or even demand. Hypersexualized advertisements and pornography depict women as simply a pair of long legs or large breasts—objects of fantasy or pleasure. But this is not the way it's supposed to be! This is a counterfeit of God's picture of sexuality. We live in a broken world, which has far-reaching effects on our physical bodies, as well as on our ideas about sex and gender. We can, however, live out our sexuality in redemptive ways. Living differently, however, begins with transforming the way we think and talk about sex.

MYTH: SEX EQUALS BEHAVIOR

When President Bill Clinton was accused of having a sexual relationship with the intern, Monica Lewinsky, in the 1990s, he turned the question "What is sex?" into a national debate. The conclusions that were drawn—in which oral sex was basically deemed "not sex"—in response to that question shocked many folks in the Christian community, and rightly so. Bill Clinton's actions and the public's response contributed to an ongoing conversation about the definition and meaning of sex.

More recently, the former Congressman Anthony Weiner became the focus of a public scandal. "Sexting" headlines were splashed across newspapers all over the country after it was revealed that Weiner had engaged in online relationships and sent partially nude photographs of himself to several women of various ages. Although Weiner eventually admitted to having inappropriate contact with at least six women online or over the phone, he reported that he had never met "or had a physical relationship with any of the women."[2] Weiner's emphasis on bodily contact belies our culture's underlying tendency to associate "sex" with physical, genital contact.

The Weiner case also highlights some of the challenges that have accompanied our increasing reliance on technology in our day-to-day communication, as well as the advent of social networking sites like Twitter and Facebook. Not only do these mediums add confusion to the already-difficult task of defining sex, they also make pornography, prostitution and sex trafficking much more easily accessible. Current technology makes all of these things immediately available—at any hour of the day or night—at the touch of a button.

Attempts to define sex, however, should not begin, or end, with the question of whether a particular *type* of sex (oral sex, phone sex, etc.) is *actually* sex. In the Clinton and Weiner controversies, the "sex" in question referred to something we do with our bodies. Although bodily sexual intimacy is a huge part of sexuality, it is certainly not the whole of it. Sexuality involves much more than that. If we want to understand why sex matters, we have to first look at who God is and how God designed us to be sexual beings.

WHAT IS SEX?

Defining sexuality is complicated. It involves who we are biologically, psychologically and socially, as well as what we do with our bodies in relationship to others. Sometimes these various aspects of sexuality are referred to as *sex* (biology and behavior) and *gender* (social and psychological identity). *Sex* and *gender* are helpful terms, but we will break those down even further to obtain a more complete picture of our identity as sexual beings. A thorough examination of what we believe about sexuality—and how we then talk about it—is necessary in order to explore how we should live as women created in God's image, designed to reflect God's loving, relational nature in our lives as gendered beings.

In order to understand sexuality in light of God's creative purpose and design, we need to go back to the very beginning. Genesis 1:26-27 states: "Then God said, 'Let us make human beings in our image.' . . . So God created human beings in his own image, / in the image of God he created them; / male and female he created them" (TNIV). From this passage we learn important, foundational truths about both who God is and who we are as humans who are made in his image. The Genesis passage describes God as saying let "us" make humans in "our" image, which is our first introduction to the trinitarian nature of God. God is one being made up of three persons, who have clear differentiation and distinction as Father, Son and Holy Spirit. Within the Trinity, we see a perfect picture of unity in diversity.

When God chose to create human beings, he could have created males only (or females only, for that matter). Instead, God chose to create males *and* females as an expression and reflection of himself as both unity (human beings) and diversity (male and female). Neither males alone nor females alone fully express who and what human beings are; the full expression of human beings is found in the unity of males and females together. Likewise, our differentiation as males and females serves to reflect the distinction of persons within the Godhead.[3] The fact that we live out our earthly lives in bodies that are distinctly male or female, then, is not incidental. Instead, it is central to what it means to be human.

For some individuals, however, life is not experienced in such a black-and-white way—in terms of being male or female. "Intersex" refers to a group of conditions where there is inconsistency between gender chromosomal assignment, anatomy, secondary sex character- istics or sex-associated hormones, like testosterone and estrogen. This inconsistency can take many forms. Some people are born with an extra sex chromosome (e.g., Klinefelter's syndrome, with an XXY) or with the absence of a chromosome (e.g., Turner's syndrome, with an XO), while others are born with inconsistency in their internal repro- ductive organs, sex chromosomes and genitals.

In addition, some babies are born with both a penis and a uterus (external male genitals and an internal female reproductive organ) in a disorder that used to be called *hermaphroditism*—though it is now being referred to as a "disorder of sex development" or "intersex" because of the confusing and pejorative nature of the former term. In the past, when a child was born with inconsistent sex characteristics, surgery was often done to make the child's external genitals appear female, which is a simpler process than creating or enlarging male genitals. The long-term consequences of this, however, have led to ethical and moral debates as those babies grew up into children or young adults who may not have identified themselves psychologically or socially as females.

Because gender is foundational to our understanding of personhood, decisions about surgical interventions in infancy or whether to raise a child with inconsistent sex characteristics as definitively male or female are important ethically and morally. The existence of intersex disorders reminds us that gender can be much more fluid than we are taught and that we need new terms to fully understand the whole spectrum of gender and sexuality. God created human beings with fundamental differences to reflect his own unity in diversity, and just as God created individuals with typical male/female characteristics in his image, so he has also created intersex individuals in his image.

To define some terms, I will refer to our essential human differentiation as *core personhood*, which encompasses *all* aspects of our sexual and gender identity—which is, in actuality, our *human* identity. Our sexuality includes a psychological, biological, sociological and behavioral component, each of which emerges from our core personhood. I imagine the foundational building blocks of our sexuality as a Venn diagram of interlocking circles (see figure 2.1), which I will refer to as *body, mind, social identity* and *behavior.* Those four circles are built on

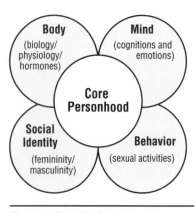

Figure 2.1. Essential Gender

Body
(biology/
physiology/
hormones)

Mind
(cognitions and
emotions)

Core
Personhood

Social
Identity
(femininity/
masculinity)

Behavior
(sexual activities)

the core personhood that God created us with to reflect God in ourselves and in our relationships. Body, mind, social identity and behavior are all intrapsychic (or internal to each person) aspects of sexuality. Of course, we are all also affected by many other factors, such as our families and our culture. These things are important in how they *impact* us, but they do not necessarily *define* us.

Body. The biological level includes our physical identity as male or female, as well as other physiological and hormonal aspects of personhood and sexuality. Our biological sex is part of who we are as embodied persons. We live out our days in male or female bodies depending on whether our fathers gave us an X or a Y chromosome at conception,[4] though this is not always so simple for some individuals.

Social identity. As men and women, most of us internally identify with those of the same biological sex and receive community recognition as being male or female. Every time I walk into a ladies' public bathroom I demonstrate this basic social identity. I am a woman, and friends and strangers alike recognize and identify me as female. For some intersex individuals, this level can be complicated as they may experience both male and female aspects of biological sex; community recognition of their identity is not as simple as it is for those with typical sex development. For individuals with gender dysphoria, who identify with members of the other biological sex, not receiving community recognition of that identification is experienced as incredibly painful. Social identity also includes how we identify with culturally held ideas about masculinity and femininity.

Mind. The psychological aspect includes our cognitions and emotions, particularly those related to our sexuality. This includes our feelings and ideas about what it means to be male or female, as well as our longings for relationship and intimacy (both romantic and otherwise) with others. The mind also includes our fantasies, which may be about an imagined, ideal romantic partner or about sexual intimacy.

Behavior. The behavioral aspect of sexuality includes all our sexually driven behaviors. Sexual activity refers to erotic or sexually charged behaviors. God created us with the capacity or potential for bodily sexual intimacy. According to a popular dictionary, *sex* refers to "sexually motivated phenomena or behavior."[5] On the behavioral level, "sex" is not equivalent to vaginal penetration. Rather, it includes a whole continuum of "sexually motivated" behaviors, which might include holding hands, kissing, caressing, touching of sexual body parts, masturbation, and oral, anal or vaginal sex. In the Clinton scandal, "sex" was reduced to vaginal penetration, which is a gross oversimplification. Vaginal penetration is only one small part of a broad spectrum of sexual behaviors and experiences.

SEX AS A SIGN

If we can agree that sex is more than just behavior, let us ask this question again in light of theological truth: What is sex? Sex is a sign. And what do signs do? They point us to something. When I direct people to my home, I alert them to the church on the corner of the main road as a sign pointing them in the direction of my home. Our bodies also function as a kind of sign. They provide a tangible, physical example of our need for relationship. The male and female anatomy fit together in a way that provides the closest kind of physical union; our bodies remind us of our fundamental incompleteness.

We were made for union with another. As Lewis Smedes points out, God created us as sexual beings with a purpose: "Male and female were created sexual to be sexual together."[6] Our bodies, however, are not merely a source of motivation toward physical relationship with another. Rather, they are a tangible reminder that God has created us *for* others and *for* God. Ultimately, we were created for union with Christ in eternity. Sexuality is the drive within us that makes us long for relationship and connection with another human and, ultimately, for union with Christ.

If sexuality provides a tangible sign and symbol of our fundamental need for relationship with others, God also uses sexuality to teach us something about *how* we should go about relating with others. Throughout the Bible, sex is used as a metaphor to explain God's relationship with his people. In the Old Testament, God is portrayed as a *lover* wooing his people. Some suggest that the erotic poetry of Song of Songs is, at least in part, an allegory describing God's love for his people. In the New Testament, the church (made up of all believers) is described as the bride of Christ. Marriage, which is where sex is located in the biblical economy, is used as the primary metaphor to understand God's love for us and union with us through Christ.

In all of these biblical images and metaphors of (sexual) love, one theme prevails: God's unfailing commitment. The Old Testament is filled with stories of God's people turning away to other gods, yet because God has made a covenant with them, his love is everlasting. He has chosen to love them and has made a commitment to them. In the book of Hosea, the metaphor of a prostitute is used to describe God's people. Despite their actions, God pursues and loves and allows his people to return to him. In the New Testament, we see a picture of commitment in Jesus' love for his disciples and followers, as the invitation for life in God is opened to all who would believe in him. Our deep longing and need for connection with others is a reflection of God's image in us, and the way God relates to us in Scripture is characterized by sacrificial love, enduring commitment and self-giving.

Sex is a sign of something eternal, which means that when our bodies come together physically, it matters. This truth can guide decisions about our sexual behavior. We can and should ask ourselves whether a given behavior is an adequate sign or reflection of the gift of eternal union with Christ to which sex is ultimately pointing. When enjoyed in the appropriate context, physical, sexual union allows us to reflect God's loving, relational nature.

This new understanding of sexuality goes beyond mere behavior, so sex can be understood as sacramental. Sexual union that takes place as God designed it to be between a husband and wife is not dismembered or dehumanized, but instead integrates all aspects of mind, body, behavior and social identity. Sacramental sex is characterized by mutual love and self-giving, which may include but is not limited to genital penetration. The covenant nature of marriage is designed to be a reflection of both God's covenant love for his people, as well as a reflection of God's own unity in diversity.

We long for union with another, and within marriage we enact the union that is to come in the one-flesh relationship with our spouse. As C. S. Lewis writes, "This is the body's share in marriage which, by God's choice, is the mystical image of the union between God and Man."[7] Whether we want it to be or not, sexual union is a sign of something else, and it *should* mean something.

The purpose of sex. Why would God use sex as a teaching tool? Theologians have long examined this question, and I will briefly describe three creational purposes of sexuality. First, sexuality is *relational*. The social nature and impact of sexual union is primary. Sexuality does not have purpose or meaning in isolation; rather, its meaning is always worked out and realized in the context of personal relationships and social institutions.[8] Sexual union functions to bond or unite two people into a one-flesh relationship, wherein each partner is called to fully share him- or herself with the other without selfishness or self-protection. Sexuality draws us into self-giving relationships with others.

Second, sexuality is *fruitful*. Sexual union provides the opportunity for people to form a particular type of relationship (parent-child) when sexual union leads to children. Contraception is so easily accessible in our time and culture that the connection between sex and procreation may seem unimportant, but to separate sex from childbearing is to ignore the most practical, mystical purpose of the sexually uniting acts. We are meant to give of ourselves in relationships in general and in particular ways within marriage. When a couple's sexual union leads to children, they open up the circle of love and commitment they share with one another to a new person. This act offers a new social role (mother or father, in addition to wife or husband), and it also allows the couple to share and give of themselves in new ways with both each other and their child.

In our culture, romantic love is so idealized that children are often portrayed as that which destroys romance. C. S. Lewis wrote, "Lovers are normally face to face, absorbed in each other,"[9] but to have children is to break the steadfast gaze on one's spouse. Once a couple has kids, popular culture seems to tell us, they no longer have any sex or fun, and thus their marriage is ruined. In a Christian understanding of marriage, having children should not destroy love but grow it up, expand it and transform it into something more mature and Christlike.

Fruitfulness, however, is not only for married, child-producing couples. Our sexuality is that which draws us to give, create, share and care for others. In later chapters, alternate expressions of fruitfulness will be introduced.

Third, sexuality is *pleasurable*. Although we may not be reminded too often of the connections between sex and procreation, our television shows and movies emphasize this third meaning exceedingly well. God created us as embodied creatures who can experience the bodily ecstasy of sexual union. The fact that we are able to experience such intense physical pleasure is not accidental; rather, God chose to create us with bodies made to give and receive pleasure in this way. The female clitoris, for example, has no functional purpose outside of pleasure. By God's creative design, the body is uniquely and intentionally created to receive pleasure in sexual activity. If you have grown up with shaming messages about your female body and sexuality, you need to read that sentence again. God created your body to experience sexual pleasure!

Some of us have grown up with images of God that are overly harsh and punitive. Perhaps we have associated God with our earthly fathers, who may have been distant or absent or even abusive. The pleasure we can experience in sexual union is a good gift from our Creator, and it should teach us about God's extravagant love for us. The biblical love poetry of the Song of Songs affirms and even celebrates the ecstasy of the pleasure that our sexuality affords. When we understand the pleasure of sexual union as a gift, we are able to understand and experience the lavishness of God's love for his people in a new way.

SEXUAL BROKENNESS

Although God chose to create us as sexual beings as a reflection of his nature, we live in a broken and fallen world. Sin has not left our sexuality untouched. Brokenness can affect all aspects of our sexuality—our minds and bodies, our sociality and our behavior. For example, Laura is a thirty-eight-year-old woman who has experienced the devastating and pervasive effects of sexual brokenness. As a child, Laura was sexually abused for several years by her grandfather, which impacted her *body*, including her physical genital organs and her hormones. Though the abuse eventually ended, Laura's shame and guilt did not, which affected her *mind*, including her thoughts and feelings. Unable to understand or accept her innocence and lack of power in the situation, Laura learned to associate femininity with sexuality, which impacted her *social identity*, including her sense of femininity. She also became sexually promiscuous at a young age, which impacted her *behavior*.

In a way, Laura's early sexual debut provided a renewed sense of power over her sexuality—power that had been taken from her as a very young girl. As time passed, however, Laura began to feel overwhelmed by guilt and shame, both for the things done to her by her grandfather as a child as well as for the things she actively participated in as a teenager and young adult. Laura began to feel like sex was the only thing she could offer in relationship, and in her longing to love and be loved, she gave that part of herself away more and more. Each experience added another brick to her growing mountain of shame and added to her self-perception as "dirty" and "damaged." Sex had become a coping mechanism for Laura, albeit an ineffective one, for managing pain and distress.

As a married adult, Laura now struggles with the sexual monotony of marriage, but she also worries about the impact of her past experiences on her husband. In addition, Laura and her husband have been trying unsuccessfully to conceive a child for several years. Their inability to do so feels to her like a personal failure, and at times, even a punishment for her past. Although she has recognized the distorted nature of her feelings about sexuality and believes cognitively that God has forgiven her for choices she made, Laura still struggles with false guilt over what was done *to* her. She cannot escape the feeling that their infertility is a result of her personal sexual brokenness. This story is a painful example of the impact of sexual brokenness on all aspects of our personhood.

Sexuality in a fallen world. And though we need to remember that sex is a gift of God, and it is good, we must also recognize that sex has been distorted and broken by the entrance of sin into the world. Sexual abuse, sexual violence and sexual addiction remind us that even what was intended for good can be used for evil. Many of us are weighed down by guilt and shame because of choices we have made about our sexual behavior.

The brokenness of our world is also evident in lingering effects on our physical, sexual bodies. Our bodies are broken, and this hard truth of life is evident in my own family where, between my mom and my mother-in-law, these women have been diagnosed with and undergone treatment for breast cancer five times. Breasts are meant for beauty, pleasure, and to nurture and sustain new life. As my mother-in-law underwent surgery for the third time last week, I could not avoid the recurrent thought that this is not the way it is supposed to be. Our fallen, broken world is evident in the devastation that has ripped through these women's bodies and our families as a result.

Brokenness may also be apparent in the way in which we experience our sexuality and gender. As previously discussed, even though we live in a binary world in which people are treated as either male or female, for some intersex individuals, gender is actually much better understood as a shade of gray. Many would suggest that gender dysphoria (when one feels and believes he or she has been assigned the wrong sex) and same-sex orientation can be understood as examples of overwhelmingly painful impacts of the fall on our lives as embodied persons.

HOPE

Our world is broken and full of pain. We all know and experience this truth to varying degrees on a daily basis. The good news, however, is that God is restoring and redeeming that which is broken. This does not mean we are promised an absence of pain, and it does not mean all of our brokenness is restored in this life. We live in a fallen world, but our hope is that we have a companion in Christ who walks with us in our struggles and loves us to our core until we are united with him in a place where the brokenness of this world is a distant memory.

So what is sex? In God's economy, sexuality should always make us more human—not less so. When our sexually motivated actions or language lead us to detach from ourselves, others or God, we know we have separated the gift of sex from the giver. The way we talk about sex matters. When men joke about "doing her," this debases both the gift of sexual union and the wholeness and integrity of females. A sacramental understanding of gender and sexuality counters the impersonal, self-centered approach represented in reductionistic descriptions, such as "doing it" or "doing her."

When I tune into television shows or overhear folks using this kind of language, I am a witness to the reality that this is not the way it's supposed to be. When I support those television shows or movies or magazines by watching or purchasing them—or if I use degrading language, even jokingly, in my own life—I become an active participant in that very brokenness. How we talk about and understand sexuality matters. Instead of listening to or using words that degrade and dehumanize, let us use language about sexuality that whispers of its God-created goodness, mystery and grace.

3

Beyond the Battle of the Sexes

*I feel that "man-hating" is an honorable
and viable political act, that the oppressed
have a right to class-hatred against
the class that is oppressing them.*

Robin Morgan,
in *Going Too Far: The Personal
Chronicle of a Feminist*

My five-year-old son, Brennan, wants to be an astronaut when he grows up (for today anyway). Last week he was jumping on the trampoline, pretending to be an astronaut catapulting into the sky, and he invited his two-year-old sister to jump with him: "Lily! I'm an astronaut, and you can be a princess!" Then he paused and looked over at me with a slight look of confusion on his face. "She can't really be a princess when she grows up, right? Then what *can* she be?"

This question made me sad, and not surprisingly, led to a mini-lecture about all the things that both boys and girls can do for a career. My little boy sees me go to work; he hears students call me "Dr. Eckert"; he kisses me goodbye when I leave town for speaking engagements; he knows I'm a writer and likes looking at the picture on the cover of my first book. He seemingly should know that little girls can grow up to do any number of professional things, and yet he has still absorbed some broader cultural message about boys and girls. Brennan's question reflects the reality that, despite years of feminism and equal rights and women's liberation movements, our kids still grow up in a very rigid, gendered world that teaches specific lessons about what is available—or not—to them as boys or girls. Growing up, we are taught in many spoken and unspoken ways what it means to be male or female. These lessons typically lead to certain expectations or ideas about what a boy does versus what a girl does, such as, "Boys should be strong and tough, and girls should be kind and sweet." Gender role expectations include the clothes we wear (pants or dresses), the sports we play (football or ballet), the roles we have in romantic relationships (pursuer or receiver), and the professions dominated by our gender (truck driver or nurse).

Gender is implicit in any conversation about sexuality, which necessarily includes body, mind, behavior and social identity. As females, we are created as sexual beings who live in particular kinds of bodies. From infancy, we are taught in subtle and not-so-subtle ways that to be human is to be a particular kind of human—a girl and then a woman. Although each of us may identify more or less closely with our surrounding culture's ideas about masculinity and femininity, these ideas shape our expectations about ourselves and others.

Sometimes these rules or lessons are so deeply ingrained in our families, churches or cultures that we struggle to distinguish between God's design and human tradition. Perhaps we were taught that gender is about power, manipulation or coercion instead of mutual support, love and respect. Thankfully, we do not need to, nor should we, look to our cultures, our families, or even our churches to discover our identity as gendered beings. Rather, we can and must find the meaning of our gender identity in and through Jesus Christ. In this chapter, I will examine two ends of the continuum on expectations about a woman's role and value, and I will suggest that we are offered a new perspective on our identity as women in Christ and how we can approach male-female relationships.

MYTH: SEXUALITY IS NOT ABOUT GENDER

When I announce that I am going to be teaching on sexuality, whether it is to a class of college students or a group of women, the expectation is almost always the same: I will be teaching about sexual behavior. As discussed in the last chapter, sexuality includes many multifaceted aspects of human personhood, but it is often reduced to only the behavioral aspect. In teaching about sexuality, before I address what we *do* with our sexual bodies, I always begin with who we *are* as sexual beings. Sexuality is ultimately always about gender, because who we are as sexual beings is men and women created in the image of God.

My identity as a sexual being is ultimately always about my identity as a *woman*. Therefore, conversations about gender are a necessary component to any comprehensive exploration of sexuality. For the remainder of this chapter, we will focus the sexuality conversation on the gender piece of the puzzle. To become sexually whole is to become a whole *woman*, but that is a confusing ideal for women today due to the contradictory messages that surround us.

One of my favorite activities to do when teaching about this is to write the following sentence stems on the board: "Women are _____ ," and "Men are _____." I ask students to call out the first things that come to mind, and we develop quite a list of characteristics. The lists are equally confusing for both men and women, but because of the nature of this book, I will focus on the themes we discuss about women.[1] Students provide descriptors that reveal a dichotomy: women should be smart, strong, sexy, assertive and independent, as well as submissive, nurturing, motherly, supportive and empathic.

In a secular feminist world, the idealized woman possesses many stereotypically masculine traits (strength, independence, drive, sexual prowess). In a conservative Christian subculture, the idealized woman is often seen as a submissive member of a patriarchal home. Which of these is the "right" view, and how do we go about making sense of our sexuality? Two recent conversations I had highlight the challenges many women face as we try to make sense of the contrasting messages we receive about what it means to be a woman.

My first conversation was with Julie, a fifty-three-year-old woman who sought counseling to deal with her husband's infidelity. Julie's husband has had a drinking problem throughout their thirty-year marriage, but Julie only recently discovered his extramarital affair. "I thought it was my job to be supportive to him no matter what," she told me in tears one day. "From the time I was a teenager, my mother instilled that lesson in me. My job was to take care of the house and the kids, and to meet his needs. So if he was stressed at work and needed a drink when he came home, I made him one. If he wanted to be intimate, I was always willing—even if I didn't feel like it or was exhausted. I feel like I've done everything right, and I am being punished. I know I have a right biblically to leave him, but what would I do? This is all I know." Julie believes her primary identity is in her role as a supportive wife, and she does not know how to respond to friends who are urging her to stand up for herself and leave her husband.

My second conversation was with Farron, a thirty-year-old single woman finishing graduate school at New York University, where she also works full time as an editor. "All of my girlfriends feel guilty for being emotional," Farron told me. Farron has been continuously struck by the double bind so many of her girlfriends are stuck in. "Independence and the image of power is something we all feel like we should attain. We should be in control but fun-loving, authoritative but with a good sense of humor, and above all, to have it appear effortless. But no woman wants to be the 'needy' woman. It is the ultimate outcast tag."

Women are faced with myriad contrasting cultural messages about who we are and what we should be as women. On one extreme are those whose experience is like Julie's: they have been taught that men are created by God to be the leaders of the home. Regardless of the husband's actions, words or attitude, the wife is expected to submit to him. In addition, wives are sometimes tacitly blamed for male misbehavior. In other words, if a husband is unfaithful, the woman may be faulted for not being affectionate enough or sexually available.

On the other extreme are those who can relate to Farron's friends, in which the ideal woman is never needy or emotional but is the epitome of independence and strength. Men are not assumed to be natural leaders and heads of home, but instead are often seen as oppressors and abusers. As this chapter's epigraph by Robin Morgan illustrates, a certain amount of anger toward men is justified and perhaps even desirable. In this chapter, I examine these dichotomous views and then turn to Christ as the ultimate model for understanding gender relationships.

THE MALE-CENTERED WOMAN

Julie loves both her parents and continues to have a close relationship with them, but she grew up in a patriarchal family, where her father worked long hours to provide financially for the family. In Julie's family, her father was strict but kind. As the clear leader of the home, he made the "final-word" decisions for the family. Julie's mom, on the other hand, managed the home as the traditional housewife — cooking, cleaning and caring for the children. She was the nurturing and supportive one.

Through a combination of unspoken messages from her family, church and community, Julie grew up believing that a woman's value lies in her identity as a wife and mother. She knew her mother was dependent on her father financially, but her mother also seemed to be dependent on her father for approval. And when her mother wanted something from her father, she would use indirect ways to get it. "He is the leader of the home and makes the final decisions," Julie's mom told her. Then, with a sly smile, her mother would add, "but I can certainly *influence* those decisions. . . . A woman has her ways!" Through all these things, Julie learned quiet but powerful lessons about manipulation.

Over time and like all of us, Julie developed particular ideas about men and women. Without intentionally doing so, Julie came to view men as superior to women. With that primary foundation, many other ideas followed. A man is the head of the home, so the woman's job is to submit to his authority. If he wants to be physically intimate, the woman should be ready and willing. "I thought it was my duty as a wife, plus I wanted to make sure his physical needs were always met to keep him from looking elsewhere." Implicit in that decision is a quiet assumption that the woman bears responsibility if the husband is unfaithful. Although Julie is angry and hurt, she has spent so many years trying to be good enough for her husband that her immediate inclination is to search for what *she* has done wrong to cause her husband to stray.

In many ways, I can relate to Julie's childhood experiences. I grew up in a conservative Christian home, and while both my parents worked outside the home once I started school, they modeled many traditional roles at home. My mom did all the cleaning and cooking, while my dad took care of the yard. At election time my dad would cut out a ballot list from the newspaper with all his selections checked for my mom to take with her to the polls. My dad was always very chivalrous with my mom—opening her car door and going out at night to fill up her car with gasoline. My mom didn't even know how to pump gasoline for many years! However, even though my dad gave my mom direction in making voting decisions, when it came to family decisions, there was no hierarchy. My parents were good friends who spent a lot of time talking to each other and making decisions about our family together.

Outside of my home, however, I learned a lot of those lessons at church that Julie had internalized. My family was always very involved there, and even as a young girl, I noticed that it was men who did all of the talking and teaching to the adults. As a young teenager I took a spiritual gifts test in which my primary gift was "pastor." I remember immediately being frustrated and asking why God would gift me with a job I couldn't do as a female. No one told me that I was not allowed to be a pastor; rather, I observed an unspoken standard in the church where the men were the leaders, with women providing the special music and teaching Sunday school or Vacation Bible School. Without even being aware of it, I came to see the church as a male-centered place in which men were valued and prized more than women.

THE FEMALE-CENTERED WOMAN

Farron lives in an urban area, dominated by ideals of women who can and should do it all. "On a bad day, it seems like everyone else makes it look so easy," she told me. "Walking a half mile in heels to get to work and looking perfectly primped while laughing on their iPhones or setting up the next meeting in an authoritative voice. Meanwhile, you feel like you can barely walk another step in your slip-ons that don't even have a heel, but they're still cutting the top of your foot. You might feel like bursting into tears, but you keep going. And the same independence that is expected in the workplace is also expected in relationships. It's not attainable."

Why do so many women feel guilty? As Farron and I began talking, we considered some of the messages that we were tacitly taught in our secular feminist educations or in other experiences. Both of us grew up outside Detroit, Michigan (a relatively liberal area of the country, particularly in comparison to the Bible Belt where I live now), and we both engaged in women's studies at liberal educational institutions (NYU for her and the University of Michigan for me). However, while Farron is single and does not have children, I am a married mother of four. Nonetheless, we both imagined ourselves becoming career women as we pursued our educations. Over time, Farron and I began to reflect on some of the messages we were taught and their impact on our identities, relationships and work.

In contrast to the patriarchy of Julie's childhood, in this more liberal, career-focused world, men were not viewed as trustworthy leaders but as oppressors and abusers. If a woman wanted to succeed professionally, she needed to be aggressive and demand power and position. To embody stereotypically masculine traits was a given. A woman's value was not in her role as a mom or wife but in her career success and ability to be totally self-reliant. This view of women translated into many areas of life. Whereas Julie learned that a woman's sexuality was to be used in service to her husband based on his needs or desires, we were taught an ethic of sexuality that suggested a woman's empowerment included sexual behavior. As a way of reclaiming power over the use of sexual coercion by men, we observed that empowered women could choose to have sex any time they wanted—on their own terms. In other words, a woman should not have sex for her husband when he wants it but for her own pleasure whenever—and with whomever—she wanted.

In both direct and indirect ways, we learned that smart women can do whatever they want and should pursue their own dreams and beliefs above all else. We were taught that a submissive woman is an unenlightened and unempowered woman. Lizz Winstead, cocreator of *The Daily Show*, is credited with coining the tagline on T-shirts and magnets that states, "I think, therefore I'm single." This equating of stupidity with relational dependence was a common one for us in the female-centered world. A woman who submits to a man sacrifices her own identity.

STUCK OR IGNORED

As both a mom and a career woman, I resonate with pieces of both Julie and Farron's stories. The mom part of me connects with Julie, because I grew up in churches and communities that idealized the quiet, gentle woman whose whole life was devoted to her husband and children. Although I wanted a career and never planned to be a stay-at-home mom, I was unprepared for how dramatically becoming a mother would alter the course of my emotional, relational and professional life. Even though I knew the research that kids with working moms do fine and even have some advantages, my priorities and goals seemed to instantaneously shift after the birth of my first child. I would have scoffed at the idea of being "just" a stay-at-home mom as a younger woman, but I began to yearn for that possibility with an almost physical hurt. The conservative argument is that kids need their mothers at home, but to be honest, I felt like the need was the other way around—with each day that passed, I was the one who needed and wanted to be home with my child.

On the other hand, the career part of me resonates with Farron and her friends. I have been academically and professionally mentored in communities that idealize the driven, aggressive woman who does not allow her children or family to deter her from success. I believe that women have amazing gifts and abilities, and that workplaces and churches miss out when women are not utilized in leadership and work. As a Christian, I believe that God called me to a particular kind of work, and that God has used me in that work. However, after my second child was born, I made a personal choice with my husband to resign from my tenure-track academic position. Although I would not change my decision, the "vocation" part of me sometimes feels guilty for putting my career on the back burner.

Furthermore, while many conservatives would applaud my decision, my professional mentors and colleagues may not. In fact, Linda Hirshman claims there is a social cost from women like me who leave the workforce to primarily be home with their children: "Their decisions are a mistake because they lead them to lesser lives, by most measures, and because these decisions hurt society. And their decision is not freely chosen, even if they 'chose' it, as it is made in the context of an ideology that assigns childrearing and housekeeping to women."[2] Hirshman argues that educated women who abandon their careers for their kids contribute to an ongoing problem of men dominating professional fields and decision-making. In other words, if I feel guilty for staying at home it is because I should—I am not being responsible to my field of study or education.

Messages like this add to the confusion. I do feel a sense of responsibility to the world around me, but I also feel responsible to my children. Hirshman suggests that leaving the workforce leads women to "lesser lives," which begs the question, what makes a life lesser or fuller? Meanwhile, the common ingredient in this equation is guilt, and I sometimes feel stuck. Currently, when I do counseling and teaching part time, I feel guilt as a mom for the time and energy I spend away from my kids, but as a psychologist who is mostly home with her kids, I feel guilty for not doing more research, training and writing in my field of study.

Recently, a student asked whether I would consider myself primarily a mom and wife *or* a professor and therapist. I immediately responded that I am a mom and wife first, but this question has stayed with me. Would that same question be asked of my husband, who is also a professor and therapist and who is also married with young children? Implicit in the question is the assumption that I must make a choice (and what kind of woman am I if I choose professor and therapist first?). Sheryl Sandberg addresses this dichotomous kind of cultural thinking in her book *Lean In*: "We need more portrayals of women as competent professionals and happy mothers—or even happy professionals and competent mothers."[3]

My story reflects my particular experience and season in life, and your story may be much different. When we examine these two extremes where a woman's value is based on her role as a mom/wife or on her professional successes, many of us are left feeling stuck or completely ignored. What about my mom's good friend Lane? She is a retired sixty-eight-year-old widow whose children are grown and live far away. In this kind of social economy, where is her value and meaning? Or perhaps you can relate to Joanie, a forty-two-year-old single woman who is unable to have children and is on disability due to a chronic and debilitating illness. Joanie doesn't have a family to care for, and her disability cut her career short. In this kind of world, where does she find her value?

When I consider the lessons that the male-centered woman or the female-centered woman teach, I see a value on externals—a woman's husband and children or her job and power. As a Christian, our value and meaning must not come from another person or object. Instead of assuming that a woman's value is based on her role (mom and wife) or her accomplishments (career success), let us turn to Jesus to examine where a woman's true value lies and how that value can and should inform our view of marriage, men, women and sex.

LET'S START OVER . . .

If our value and identity as women is not in our roles or accomplishments, where can it be found? One problem we face when confronting complicated and polarizing issues, such as gender, identity and value, is that we often begin with ourselves. We have already come to some kind of conclusion and merely want our theology to confirm it. We have *already* decided how we think men and women ought to behave and relate, and *then* we use Scripture or doctrine to support our beliefs. This is backwards. We have to begin with God at the center. We must first ask who God is, and then examine the implications for our human identities and relationships. After reading and reflecting on God's character, I am going to suggest three central principles that can guide our understanding of gender relations: unity and difference, order and equality, and loving relations.

Unity and difference. We worship one God (unity) in three persons: Father, Son and Spirit (difference). God created human beings (unity) in God's own image as males and females (difference). In Galatians 3:28 we are told, "There is neither Jew nor Gentile, neither slave nor free, nor is there male and female, for you are all one in Christ Jesus." This verse does not mean Christ erased gender distinctions and intends for us all to be the same. Rather, gender is the way in which God has chosen to express his unity in diversity in the Trinity, and it is good! In other words, it matters very much that we are male and female because God chose to create us this way as a reflection of himself. Men and women together reflect God's character. But Galatians 3:28 makes it clear that, as Gordon Fee points out, *"value and identity* based on gender, especially with regard to societal structures and roles, are now a thing of the past for the people of God."[4]

Order and equality. The Son is always the Son (order) but is also fully God (equality); the Father is always the Father but is also fully God; the Spirit is always the Spirit but is also fully God. Men and women are not different primarily in our gender roles, nor in the power or authority we hold. Just as the primary difference among the Father, Son and Holy Spirit is not one of power or authority or role (Father, Son and Spirit are all fully God), so men and women's differences are not essentially about power or authority or prescribed gender roles.

Everything I do, I do *as a woman.* When I speak to my husband or nurture my children, I do so as a woman. When I experience anger or sadness or grief, I do so as a woman. This does not mean I always think or behave in stereotypically feminine ways. However, even when I am speaking assertively (a stereotypically masculine trait), I do so as a woman. Conversely, when my husband nurtures me, he does so *as a man.* In our relationship, I give what only I can give, and I receive what I cannot give myself. The same is true for my husband. Within this order and equality, we experience two different sides of love.

Loving relations. The Father, Son and Spirit are constantly giving and receiving love to and from one another. The Father gives and receives love as the Father; the Son gives and receives love as the Son; and the Spirit gives and receives love as the Spirit. God is constantly reaching out and giving love to us. God is always self-giving and self-revealing. So what if submission is really about a willingness to receive? God wants us to receive his love, and pride keeps us from receiving from God what we cannot give ourselves.

Our differences as men and women should not be used as a means of self-protection, self-promotion or personal advantage. Rather, those differences should be used to honor the other. If we are to interpret our identities as sexual beings (both who we are as male and female, and how we live in these bodies) in light of the new creation, then we must follow Christ's example: During his time on earth, Jesus held ultimate power yet did not lord his power over others. Instead, as Judy and Jack Balswick write, "Jesus modeled a new way of being personally powerful. He rejected the use of power to control others but used power to serve others, to lift up the fallen, to encourage responsibility and maturity."[5]

If we are to reflect God's character in our relationships, then we should use whatever power we have to encourage and love one another. We have a better alternative than either the male-centered or female-centered ideals, in which our value is found primarily in our roles or accomplishments. Instead, the centered woman lives with Christ as her center, which informs her relationships and work (see table 3.1).

This Christ-centered model is intended to provide a reminder of who we are as women who are created in God's image, not to serve as another unattainable standard of perfection. As women, we do not need anything else to help us feel guilty, but what we *do* need is mentors and models of how to honor God as women in our bodies, our work and our relationships. I hope that this model can provide a vision that is in direct contrast to the way things so often *are* when it comes to gender expectations and male-female relationships—creating a vision for how things *could* be in God's redemptive design.

Table 3.1.

	MALE-CENTERED View of Women	CHRIST-CENTERED View of Women	FEMALE-CENTERED View of Women
Primary identity	Wife and mother	Child of God, sister in Christ, co-image-bearer (informs relationships, parenting and work)	Independent woman (successful career, financial and emotional self-reliance)
Important traits to embody	Stereotypically feminine (nurturing, empathic, quiet, gentle, motherly, etc.)	Both stereotypically masculine and feminine traits that uniquely reflect God's image	Stereotypically masculine (strong, self-reliant, aggressive)
How we attain power	Indirectly— through manipulation, sex, passive-aggressive behavior	Directly— through genuinely and authentically sharing feelings and directly asking for needs to be met	Aggressively— through dominating or demanding for rights and power
	MALE-CENTERED View of Men	CHRIST-CENTERED View of Men	FEMALE-CENTERED View of Men
Superiority	Men are viewed as superior to women	Men and women equally bear the image of God and are co-mandated to care for the earth	Women are viewed as superior to men
Men's natural tendencies	Natural, ascribed leaders and heads of home	Men are gifted in unique ways but also carry unique wounds	Abusers and oppressors
	MALE-CENTERED View of Sex	CHRIST-CENTERED View of Sex	FEMALE-CENTERED View of Sex
Purpose	For the husband (and a wife's duty is to meet her husband's needs)	For the mutual giving and receiving of pleasure in marriage	For self (for a woman looking to meet her own needs)
When and where	In marriage, primarily based on husband's desire	In covenant marriage when mutually desirable	Whenever and wherever a woman chooses
	MALE-CENTERED Male-Female Relationships	CHRIST-CENTERED Male-Female Relationships	FEMALE-CENTERED Male-Female Relationships
Relational Consequence	Female dependency	Male-female interdependence	Male emasculation

THE CHRIST-CENTERED WOMAN

As Christ-centered women, we are grounded in our identities as human beings created in God's image. As such, we have been given a mandate to care for the earth and to reflect or image God's character. The lens through which we view our activities, roles and responsibilities is not as a career woman or as a mom or wife, but rather, is as a child of God. As such, you or I may be a mother, sister, daughter, teacher, friend, nurse, doctor and so on, and we may engage in any number of activities, such as changing diapers or making coffee, doing research or meeting clients, cooking dinner or making presentations. We may be old or young, married or single. Our value remains the same. These activities, roles and relationships do not define us; Christ defines us.

Christ mediates all our relationships and activities. Therefore, as Christ-centered women, we no longer need to vie for power through aggression and dominance, nor do we need to manipulate people into doing what we want through passive-aggressive behavior or other indirect methods. Rather, we can be genuine and authentic in relationships. We can directly share our feelings and ask for our needs to be met, even as we look for ways to give love and meet others' needs.

With Christ as our model and mediator, we can rest in the God-given personality traits we have and seek those that better reflect God's loving nature. The fruit of the Spirit is not divided by gender, in which women are supposed to be "good" and men are supposed to be "patient." Rather, the fruit of the Spirit is a model for us all. Gender does not define the shape of love. "Love is patient, love is kind. It does not envy, it does not boast, it is not proud. It does not dishonor others, it is not self-seeking, it is not easily angered, it keeps no record of wrongs. Love does not delight in evil but rejoices with the truth. It always protects, always trusts, always hopes, always perseveres" (1 Corinthians 13:4-7). This portrait of love is not a gendered ideal for either men or women. I long to embody these traits with my husband and my children, my friends and my neighbors. As a wife, I protect my husband as a woman, and he protects me as a man. These are two sides of one loving relationship. He protects and loves me in a way I cannot do myself, and I protect and love him in a way he cannot do himself.

This alternative to a male-centered or female-centered perspective also has implications for how we view men. In contrast to either idealizing or demeaning men, a Christ-centered approach sees men in a more holistic manner. Men essentially carry the same gifts and burdens as women, even as we experience the world in often drastically different ways (because of upbringing, culture, hormones, personal experiences, etc.). Men and women are both created in God's image, and we are therefore equally mandated to care for the world and to reflect God in our lives, work and relationships. Men are not our enemies (a consequence of male emasculation) or our saviors (a consequence of female dependency); they are our brothers in Christ. Like us, they have struggles and weaknesses, but they should not be defined by those. Rather, their value lies in their identities as men created in God's image.

In light of this view of men and woman as co-image-bearers, who are called to give and receive love, sexual choices and behaviors are no longer pursued as a means to an end. Pleasure is not pursued for pleasure's own sake whenever one feels desire, nor does one use sex to coerce or placate another. Rather, sexually motivated behavior in general is a reflection of giving to another what they cannot give themselves, and receiving from another what we cannot give ourselves. Genital sexual behavior, in particular, is reserved for the covenant marriage and based on an equal valuing of each partner's needs, feelings and desires. It is an intimacy of whole selves, not mere bodies.

If we have a vision for sexual wholeness, we must make sure that vision does not simply focus on the behavioral aspects of sexuality. Too often, discussions of sexuality are focused exclusively on what our bodies *do* instead of what our bodies *mean* and who we *are*—as human beings who live and breathe and pray and talk and speak in those particular bodies. Our value is not in whether we are married or single. It is not about our husband's income or our children's accomplishments. Nor are we valuable because of how successful we are in our careers or volunteerism. Rather, sexual wholeness and restoration comes in and through Christ alone.

For many of us, finding our identity in Christ is difficult because of all the ways in which we have learned about our value and worth as women and as sexual beings. Growing up in American culture, we are offered vivid messages about women and sexuality. In the next chapter, we will examine the power of some of those lessons.

4

Sexual Self-Image in a Girls-Gone-Wild World

*A baseline expectation that women will be constantly
exploding in little blasts of exhibitionism runs
throughout our culture. Girls Gone Wild
is not extraordinary, it's emblematic.*

Ariel Levy,
Female Chauvinist Pigs:
Women and the Rise of Raunch Culture

*Instead of fulfilling the promise of infinite orgastic bliss,
sex in the America of the feminine mystique is becoming
a strangely joyless national compulsion, if not a contemptuous
mockery. The sex-glutted novels become increasingly explicit
and increasingly dull; the sex kick of the women's magazines
has a sickly sadness. . . . American women have turned their
attention to the exclusive, explicit, and aggressive pursuit of
sexual fulfillment, or the acting-out of sexual phantasy.*

Betty Friedan,
The Feminine Mystique

When Alyssa walked into my office for the first time, I was a bit taken aback. I knew from our initial phone conversation that she was coming to counseling for help with self-esteem and body image. The person who stood before me, however, was one of the most beautiful women I had ever seen. I should not have been surprised because the connection between self-image and actual appearance is not strong. Despite the belief that, if we could just lose ten pounds or have thicker hair, we would be happy and confident, the truth is that confidence is not related to actual appearance.

Alyssa was a great example of this. At twenty-seven years old, she had flawless skin, striking features, and a body that had been sculpted with years of dieting and religious exercise. Every day when Alyssa got out of the shower, she would analyze her naked body in front of the mirror, searching for and critiquing any perceived imperfections. Despite Alyssa's appearance, she never felt pretty enough or sexy enough and was plagued by internal self-loathing and insecurity. Alyssa had had many romantic relationships and felt inadequate in the area of sexuality as well: "I'm just never enough for them." In an effort to please past boyfriends, Alyssa sometimes participated in physically uncomfortable or sexually degrading acts. "That's what guys want," she told me. "It's what they expect, and I guess it's not that big of a deal."

Alyssa had been learning about what it means to be a woman for her entire life. Like her, we learn these lessons directly and indirectly from our parents and siblings, our friends and neighbors, our colleagues and bosses. In more subtle ways, however, we absorb lessons about personhood through popular culture. We live in a media-saturated world, and those sources flood us with images of women and sex. They offer us a picture of women and sexuality that can drastically affect our sexual self-image — how we think and feel about ourselves as sexual creatures. We are all consumers, to some degree, of the culture around us. Whether we are conscious of it or not, when we take in media, we also consume lessons about womanhood and sexuality. Alyssa had internalized many of those ideals about how women should look and act; in our counseling together, we began to unpack some of the subtleties of those messages and how they had affected her feelings and behavior.

MYTH: WHAT OUR CULTURE TEACHES ABOUT WOMEN AND SEXUALITY IS TRUE

Several years ago MTV was under attack for a scripted show, *Skins*, whose focus was explicit depictions of teenage sexual behavior and drug use. Though it was cancelled after only one season, it was not the first controversial show on MTV. In 1999, the MTV show *Undressed* debuted and ran for six seasons, exploring the sexual relationships of older teens and twenty-somethings. Many Americans challenged the appropriateness of these shows, as well as the idea that they were truly representative of typical teen and young-adult sexual behavior. If we believe what we see on MTV, then we are living in a world in which our lives are centered around sex and a constant cycle of promiscuous behavior and sexual partners. Those shows were meant to be racy and extreme, but similar ideas infiltrate other kinds of media in more subtle ways. Is it possible that we are being barraged with the *Skins* and *Undressed* messages without being aware of them?

MTV is not the first cultural medium to offer a hypersexualized depiction of human relationships. In the second epigraph of this chapter, Betty Friedan is quoted in her classic feminist manifesto, *The Feminine Mystique*, where she challenged the hypersexualization of the 1960s culture. Cultural lessons about women and sexuality are not new, but the ways we receive them in our technological age differ from the experiences of our mothers and grandmothers.

This morning when I turned on my computer to check my email and say hello to a friend on Facebook, I had to navigate through several pop-up advertisements, some of which featured suggestive comments and lingerie-clad women. When I opened my email account, I had a message from "Sexy Partners" with a subject line that read: "Kimgaineseckert: Find sex partners in your area." Like many of you, I get messages like this so often that my eyes skim right over them.

And while waiting in line at the grocery store, I can't flip through a magazine without being flooded by ads featuring scantily dressed women in sexually provocative poses. When I watch TV, I am bombarded with commercials where sex is used to sell everything from diamonds to vacuum cleaners—and even hamburgers! The fast-food chain Hardee's has gained notoriety for its commercials that are so hypersexualized that they are being called misogynistic by critics. When I think about a typical day, the amount of media I am exposed to is extensive. To be honest, I sometimes feel so desensitized to the images I see of women everywhere—the sexualization of women in advertising, television and movies—that I don't even notice them.

But not noticing can be a dangerous thing. Last week I was driving a familiar route to a friend's home with my kids. Across the street from the intersection where we were stopped was a stark, windowless eyesore of a building with large, pink fluorescent letters advertising "Adult Books." As we waited for the light to turn green, my beginning-reader son called out proudly from the backseat, "Mom! That's a place for adult books!" The paradox of the innocent pride in his voice and the rundown house of brokenness in front of me almost brought tears to my eyes. When I had first driven by that store many years ago, I had felt a wave of anger and frustration, but over time, it began to blur into the background so that I had almost forgotten it was there. Just like I had stopped noticing the adult bookstore, many of us have stopped noticing hypersexualized images of women surrounding us.

In this chapter, I will attempt to counteract this kind of not noticing. In Romans 12:2, Paul tells us not to become so well-adjusted to our culture that we fit into it without even thinking: "Instead, fix your attention on God. You'll be changed from the inside out. Readily recognize what he wants from you, and quickly respond to it. Unlike the culture around you, always dragging you down to its level of immaturity, God brings the best out of you, develops well-formed maturity in you" *(The Message).* Our culture offers vivid lessons about women and sexuality, and when we internalize those lessons from the advertising and entertainment industries, they can dramatically impact our sexual behavior—as well as how we think and feel about ourselves as women. They do not, however, reflect the truth of who we are as women created in God's image, nor do they accurately depict the beauty of sexuality as God designed it.

SELLING WOMEN

One of my favorite classes to teach at the Christian college where I work part time is a seminar on the psychology of women. Many of my students have grown up in a particular conservative subculture where traditional ideas about gender have been passed down to them. These same students live in a media-saturated world of constant exposure to advertising and entertainment. Without making a conscious choice to do so, my students have internalized very specific ideas about what it means to be a girl or a woman.

One of my first assignments for this class is intended to help them become more mindful of the advertising they absorb in their media consumption, as well as alert them to the underlying lessons being taught in such advertising. To do so, I ask students to bring three different print advertisements to class: one ad that contains pictures of women only, one with men only, and one ad with men and women together. As students arrive, we post the ads on different walls of the classroom so an entire wall of advertisements is of women, one of men, and one of both men and women. I then ask students to slowly walk around the room, study the ads, and take notes on any themes or patterns they observe. "If you took all your lessons about what it means to be a woman from these ads, what would you learn?" I ask. Year after year, several patterns emerge, so I will briefly describe four of the most pervasive and consistent themes.

Woman as (sexualized parts of) a body. Every year my "women only" wall is flooded with advertisements depicting pictures of *parts* of women's bodies, especially the sexualized parts of the female body like lips or buttocks, breasts or legs. A jeans company features a naked woman's lower back (where are the jeans?). A liquor ad contains a close-up shot of a woman's breasts, shoulders and mouth (but no eyes). Women's bodies, but not women themselves, are used to sell everything from perfume to clothing to cars.

Woman as (nonliving) object. "What's in your martini?" is the tagline in an ad featuring a woman in a bikini inside a giant martini glass. Variations of this theme—where women are depicted as things to be consumed—are common. Another ad features a famous model whose makeup is so heavy, and whose expression is so vacant, that she is almost unrecognizable. When real women are depicted as things— consumable objects or plastic mannequins—we learn important lessons about a woman's (lack of) value.

Woman as (provocative) little girl or little girl as woman. Another common theme students observe is advertisements with the juxtaposition of adult women dressed in provocative childish clothing (like baby-doll dresses that are low-cut and reveal adult breasts) or engaging in sexualized yet childish activities like sucking on candy or a lollipop. One particularly disturbing ad from a prestigious car company features a close-up of the face and naked shoulders of a teenage-looking girl, gazing seductively at the camera. The tagline reads, "You know you're not the first." The ad is reminiscent of the sixteen-year-old Britney Spears music video, "Baby One More Time." With her provocative dance moves, facial expressions, and her low-cut, belly-baring, Catholic-school uniform, Spears looked like a cross between a precocious girl and a stripper. The blurring of boundaries between child and woman is a dangerous one. Consider this disturbing statistic: in one year, 28,000 men paid for sex with adolescent girls.[1] When we blur the boundaries between girls and women, it teaches us to both sexualize children and infantalize women.

Woman as sexually submissive or **woman as sexual victim.** Some of the most shocking ads depict women in positions of clear sexual subservience. A high-end fashion company features a woman lying face down across a man's lap with his hand poised over her buttocks—apparently having just spanked her. A vodka ad depicts an almost-naked woman lying on the beach with a fully-dressed man standing over her, one leg on each side of her breasts. A popular clothing brand shows a woman dressed in lingerie, lying on her back, with a blank expression on her face, and it is unclear whether she is vacant (dissociative) or sexually aroused. Further, a partially naked man is positioned over her, while several other half-dressed men surround her. Whenever I ask students what they see in this ad, the most consistent answer is rape. These ads are frightening because they link sexuality and violence. What does it mean for us as a culture if sexual violence is being used—successfully—to sell a product? We should not be surprised by the prevalence of pornography, prostitution or trafficking of minors when we see the ways in which women and sexual violence are being used to sell products.

After visually scanning the room, filled with advertisements, the differences in the sexualization of women versus men is undeniable. Furthermore, my students also consistently remark on the "expert" theme in the advertisements featuring only men. We frequently see ads with men as doctors or chefs, giving important advice or information about health, wellness, food, cookware and so on. And, in ads that feature men and women together, students notice that women are typically depicted as dominating the home and family sphere, with fathers off in the background.

I invite you, the next time you see a print advertisement or a commercial, to take a moment to pay attention to how women are being portrayed. Consider how these images have affected your own self-image over time. When you look at advertisements in magazines, how do you feel about yourself? Most women feel worse. And that is the point, isn't it? If we feel bad about ourselves, then the obvious solution is to buy the product being sold to make us feel better. As you begin paying more attention to the background messages, consider how these pictures make you feel as a sexual being.

A poor body image can have a drastic affect on our comfort in being sexually intimate with another person. If you are basing your worth and value on what you see in ads or commercials, how do you measure up? What should you be doing or not doing in your bedroom? Years of exposure to hypersexualized images of women set up false expectations for both men and women about what women should look like and act like, and both husbands and wives can end up feeling disappointed with reality if they are buying into the lies of our culture.

Alyssa shared a poignant story about going to the beach with a boyfriend that illustrates her constant sense of disappointment with her appearance. When she walked out in a bikini, he said, "That makes me think of a three-letter word!"

Alyssa immediately responded, "Fat?"

Of course, the word he was thinking of was *sex*, but Alyssa was so fixated on her bodily imperfections she assumed he was thinking about those as well.

For many of us, the reason these ads have faded into the background is because we have seen them for so long. But what about our daughters, nieces or granddaughters? The potential impact on young girls who are growing up in a world saturated with these images is startling. My client Alyssa loved fashion magazines and had been poring over issues of *Vogue* and *Cosmo* since she was a teenager. Years of comparing herself to unrealistic, airbrushed images of women had left her with a baseline feeling of inadequacy; regardless of her actual appearance, there was always something wrong that needed to be fixed. In addition, the constant exposure to hypersexualized women influenced Alyssa's thoughts and feelings about her expected behavior with men. According to her, the women she idealized were physically "perfect," and part of their appeal was their overt sexual appearance and behavior. Yet after years of emulating these images in both her appearance and behavior, Alyssa still felt lonely, sad and inadequate.

Of course, the sexualized messages of advertising do not just impact girls and women. Advertisements tell a story about what women are and what they want, and that story is often being told to men. Take some time to flip through a men's magazine, and then consider the effects these seductive and powerful messages about women can have on male consumers. If boys and men are trying to understand women, the lessons offered in advertising teach men to have very particular expectations about women. Many women can relate to Alyssa, who felt like she could never be beautiful or sexy enough to satisfy any man.

Advertising sells women, and when we buy into those messages, it can have a dramatic impact on how we think and feel about ourselves as sexual beings. When women are consistently being sold—as parts of a body, as nonliving objects, as sexually submissive victims or as provocative little girls—it affects us all. We are all consumers of media to a greater or lesser degree, and we must learn to be thoughtful and critical consumers. God created women not to be merely objects of sexual fantasy; rather, we are image-bearers who have been uniquely gifted in specific ways. This is who we are in God's economy, and healing takes place as we begin to notice and reject the lies in popular culture about a woman's worth. Instead, we can find value in both ourselves and others in the things that matter most: our ability to relate authentically, care for the earth, and use our talents to serve God and each other.

SELLING SEX

Most of us don't intentionally consume advertising, but we do actively seek out entertainment. We go to the movies with friends or on dates; we DVR our favorite shows; we subscribe to services like Netflix or Hulu so we can instantly watch our desired programming. Our digital cable or satellite television services offer hundreds of stations to choose from at any time. If we don't find what we are looking for there, we simply go online to find more shows and movies. We are an entertainment-obsessed culture, and the television programming and movies released in our country are saturated with sexual behavior. *Skins, Undressed* and *Girls Gone Wild* are extreme examples of an industry that is hypersexualized. From the sexual innuendos in children's programming to the open promiscuity of many reality shows, our entertainment industry paints an explicit picture of sexuality. Porn star Jenna Jameson's publisher describes this raunchiness as representative of what she calls a "porno-ization of the culture."[2]

In this section, we will examine several specific lessons that are being taught by our "porno-ized" culture. What we often see in the entertainment industry's depiction of sexuality is an attempt to remove the behavioral and biological components of sexuality (hormones, arousal and physical acts) from the other aspects of sexuality (sociality, cognitions and emotions)—and to completely detach sex from our core personhood. If we believe what we see on TV and in the movies, we may be led to think that sex can be "just sex," or that we can detach sexual behavior from the emotional, the relational and the spiritual. All of these components, however, are created by God to be inherently interconnected in a holistic sexuality.

Hypersexual behavior is good. One of the most disturbing messages communicated in popular culture is that experimental, explorative, promiscuous sexual behavior that is disconnected from emotional and relational commitment is the norm. Sex is a god to be pursued above all else. If we are learning what it means to be a sexually healthy adult from watching television or movies, then we are learning that sexual behavior is merely a release of impulse, desire or need; it is disconnected and even dehumanized. This distortion of sex as mere behavior is in direct contrast to God's creative work in sexuality. Sexual union is a gift created by God, drawing people together in a one-flesh relationship. Although physical pleasure in sexual behavior is also a gift from God, it is never meant to be *just* a physical act. Consequences ensue when we try to dismember sexual behavior from relationship and from what sex means as it reflects something of the character of God.

Sex equals penetration. This disconnected view of sexuality also leads to a compartmentalized view of sexual behavior. When physical, sexual acts become disconnected from relationship and personhood, "virginity" becomes a technical term equated primarily with (lack of genital) penetration. In our counseling, I asked Alyssa to write her sexual autobiography—to tell her story of sexuality, including how she learned about sexuality, her earliest thoughts and feelings about it, as well as her sexual experiences over time.

Alyssa's confusion regarding herself as a sexual being was evident throughout the story, and one example of this was in her use of the term *virgin*. As an adolescent, Alyssa began performing oral sex on boys at their request. She engaged in sexual exploration of genitals and mutual masturbation with boys throughout high school, yet she stated that she remained a virgin until she was twenty-one years old.

Alyssa is not alone in equating sex with penetration. In a 2003 study, surveying college students at Northern Kentucky University who had signed sexual abstinence commitment cards, 21 percent had engaged in oral sex but didn't consider it to be "sex."[3] Only when Alyssa had experienced vaginal penetration did she believe she had "lost" her virginity. The whole concept of "losing" one's virginity is, in itself, telling. Sexual behavior is on a continuum, and it is meant to be something we share and give to another in a covenant relationship—not something we inadvertently lose to a temporary partner. When we try to remove specific sexual acts from the whole picture of sexuality, we miss out on the real purpose and beauty of sexuality.

Sex is for the young and beautiful. Imagine that you have just gone into your living room and turned on the television. As you flip through the channels, you inevitably stumble on a steamy sex scene. Take a moment to get a picture in your mind of what the actors and actresses in those scenes look like. Are they elderly folks who have been married for forty years? Are they middle-aged, overweight or just plain average looking? Probably not. In 2012, the movie *Hope Springs*, starring Tommy Lee Jones and Meryl Streep, made waves because of its explicit focus on the sexual relationship of an older married couple. This movie was noteworthy because it moved away from the typical message our culture sends about sexuality—that only young and beautiful people are (or should be) having sex.

Contrary to the "young and beautiful" myth, we are all sexual— whether young or old, male or female, single or married. Of course, the Hollywood idea that the only people engaging in sexual behavior are young and beautiful is inaccurate and absurd. But this message goes even deeper. As females and males created in God's image, we are all sexual beings, whether we are "having sex" or not. We express our sexuality through our longings for God and others from our earliest moments of life. We are sexual, and not merely when we are acting on urges related to physical, sexual desires. We are sexual in all the ways in which we live in female or male bodies, and in all the ways in which we long for connection with others.

Boys will be boys. Television and movies also offer a disturbing caricature of men as animalistic creatures who are always and only thinking about sex, who will have sex with whoever they can, whenever they can. Women are literally objects to receive their need for sexual release. If we believe the media portrayals, then this is just the way men are, and women need to accept that all men will lust, masturbate and look at pornography.

Several years ago, the popular sitcom *Friends* illustrated this theme in an episode where one of the main characters, Monica, walked in on her husband, Chandler, after he had been watching pornography and masturbating. Chandler was embarrassed and quickly switched the channel to an educational program on sharks when she walked in. The show follows Monica as she processes her fears and concerns that her husband is sexually aroused by "shark porn." Her concern is neither with the masturbation, nor with the "regular" porn—presumably because both of those things are so normal and to be expected. In other words? Boys will be boys.

If we believe the media portrayals of sex as a god to be pursued and as a physiological need that we have to release periodically, then sexual partners become not people but objects—a physical place to release our need. Sexual behavior becomes a self-serving pursuit of physical pleasure, rather than a place to give of self to another—as a reflection of how God is in a constant self-giving and receiving relationship in the Trinity.

Good girl or *bad girl (Madonna/whore)*. If we learn from popular culture that boys will be boys, what do we learn about girls? Black-and-white lessons about female sexuality abound, and the old Madonna/whore archetype still exists. In the Grammy-winning hip-hop song "Yeah," Usher applauds and reflects this kind of dichotomous thinking when he sings about wanting a "lady on the street" but a "freak in the bed."[4] In this reductionistic view, women are either good girls who are chaste or bad girls who desire sex all the time. Good girls may be alternately idealized for their morality and motherliness or ridiculed for their frigidity and naivete. Bad girls may be sexually sought after by males while also being the target of gossip and name-calling (e.g., what is the male equivalent of the term *slut*?).

In the current cultural climate, the ancient whore archetype is evident in the increasingly common portrayal of female characters being just like men in their sexual drive to experience physical sexual pleasure at all costs. It is not only on MTV where we see this kind of sexual attitude. Popular primetime shows of the last decade, such as *Sex and the City* or *Desperate Housewives*, are filled with female characters who are promiscuous or even sexually exploitive, using sex and their bodies to hurt someone else (a jealous friend) or get ahead professionally (sleeping with the boss).

Historically, the stereotypical Madonna archetype was exemplified by the one-dimensional mothers on television sitcoms, such as Mrs. Cleaver or even Mrs. Brady. These characters were not women; they were *mothers*. While they were to be respected and adored, they were not sexually desired! In today's culture, we see the Madonna archetype persist in female characters who are uncomfortable with their bodies or with sexual behavior. A recent example of the good girl stereotype is Emma, the guidance counselor on the popular musical television series *Glee*, whose OCD mandates that she individually washes her grapes and is unable to consummate a marriage. Cultural ideas about sexuality are particularly striking in Emma's character, where her virginity is portrayed as a direct result of her mental illness. In the Madonna archetype, good girls are not sexual girls.

Andrea, a thirty-two-year-old woman I saw in counseling, had been married for six years, and she reported a lack of intimacy and sexual desire in her marriage. According to Andrea, she and her husband had been sexually active before marriage. At that time, her desire was high and their sexual relationship was satisfying, except for the guilt she felt because she was convicted that sexual intimacy should be saved for marriage. After Andrea and her husband got married, her sexual desire and their overall marital intimacy gradually changed. She continued to engage in sexual activity with her husband whenever he initiated it, but his interest had decreased as well after they got married. Throughout their marriage, her husband has refused to be sexually intimate in any way when she menstruates, not even wanting to kiss or embrace her. He stopped initiating sexual intimacy when she became pregnant, because of his fears of hurting the baby and his discomfort with her growing body. After the birth of their first child, Andrea's husband told her he had a hard time feeling sexual toward her now that she was breastfeeding.

All of these things reveal the subtle ways that the good girl/bad girl thinking can infiltrate our day-to-day living. Andrea's husband had a difficult time reconciling his notion of her as a bad girl (the single woman who was sexually interested all the time) and as a good girl (the mother of his child). In the bad girl mentality, a woman's body is to be used for sex. In the good girl mentality, a woman's body is to be used for childbearing. In both, the woman's body is an object. Neither of these archetypes allows for a woman to be a healthy, whole person where sexual behavior is interwoven with the body, mind and spirit.

No doesn't mean no. Shortly after getting married, my husband and I saw a movie that was disturbing, but unfortunately, involved a scenario that is repeated in movies over and over. In this scene, the male and female lead characters get into a heated argument. The man and woman are both physically attractive and the tension between them, which is sexual in nature of course, is palpable. The argument becomes more heated until, suddenly, the man grabs the woman, pushes her up against the wall and kisses her aggressively. At first she resists, saying "No, no, no," and she pushes him away. The pushing away and verbal requests to stop, however, gradually morph into sexually responsive behavior, where she is saying no while pulling him toward her. Ultimately, the scene ends with them having seemingly ecstatic sexual intercourse.

What happens when an inexperienced sexual boy watches this movie? What does he learn about sex in general and female sexual cues in particular? If our media culture's lessons are accurate—that we are all hypersexual, that sexual behavior can be disconnected from the deeper meaning of sexuality, that boys will be boys, and that women are either sexually promiscuous or frigid—then sexual assault, rape and unwanted sexual activity will be a natural result in this climate. These kinds of scenes teach us to believe that women really do "want it" all the time, but we are either gamey (promiscuous) or we don't know how to behave (frigid). Either way, the message is that men should press on when women say no.

The research being done on sexual violence supports the reality that we live in a world dominated by this kind of thinking. According to RAINN (the Rape, Abuse and Incest National Network), one in six American women will be the victim of rape or attempted rape in her lifetime. In research studies examining unwanted sexual experiences, the results confirm these estimates. Almost 78 percent of female college students in one study reported a history of unwanted sexual activity.[5] Another study of college females at religious schools found that over half reported at least one unwanted sexual incident in their history.[6] In a study of over 6,000 college women, 54 percent report having experienced some kind of sexual aggression or victimization, and 27 percent of those reported having experienced rape.[7]

These statistics are overwhelming. Sadly, the stories I hear in my counseling practice support these numbers. Not only that, but I fear that many women have begun to "not notice" sexual assault, even (or perhaps especially) when it happens to them.

Linda was a thirty-five-year-old woman who came to see me for counseling for depression. When I asked her if she had any history of sexual abuse at our first meeting, she immediately said no. At our second meeting, however, Linda almost casually mentioned that she had experienced a "date rape situation in college." Similarly, Jackie, a married woman in her thirties who was seeing me for help in her marriage, also initially denied any sexual assault or abuse. In our third session, however, she disclosed that her husband had forced her to have sex on numerous occasions when he was intoxicated.

When sexual assault against women has become so common that women do not recognize it as such, that is a serious problem indeed.

THE IMPORTANCE OF NOTICING

When I ask my students to begin noticing the underlying messages in the advertising, television and movies they consume, I find that I, too, begin attending to these messages with new eyes. Too often, we assume that people understand the portrayals of women and sexuality in these places as caricatures, as extremes, as *non*reality. So we don't notice the potential dangers. Or perhaps we see the risks, but we fear what others will think if we actively respond. In light of this conversation, we might be tempted to chastise ourselves or others: *It's just an ad*, or *it's just a movie* or *don't overreact*, we tell ourselves. Is it possible, however, that some boys, girls, women and men *are* buying into the messages being sold, perhaps without even being aware of it?

If I asked Alyssa whether she thought women were meant to be hypersexualized objects to be consumed by men, she would be offended and upset. Yet her beliefs about herself and her behavior with men tell a different story. Without being conscious of it, Alyssa has internalized some damaging messages about what she should look like and do as a woman. Even when we know these portrayals of women and sexuality are inaccurate, many of us still struggle with feeling like we are not beautiful or sexy enough.

When the messages being offered in our media-saturated world about women are this disturbing, I believe we pay a price for *not* noticing. Clearly, in a very tangible way, some folks *are* believing what they are seeing, so we should not be surprised by the reality that some of our neighbors, colleagues and church members are involved in the consumption of pornography, prostitution and other forms of sexual exploitation of women.

Begin to inventory the kinds of unspoken messages that you, your friends, your daughters, sons and spouses are being exposed to through advertising, television and movies. Because when we fail to notice, we are unable to respond. Noticing is empowering; it enables us to be active and thoughtful consumers and women. We can highlight and discuss the inaccuracies and falsehoods in these images with our spouses, friends, daughters and sons. We can make choices about which products to buy, which magazines to support with our readership and funds, which movies and TV shows to watch. But first, we have to notice!

5

The Shame of Silence

For you were once darkness, but now you are light
in the Lord. Live as children of light (for the fruit
of the light consists in all goodness, righteousness
and truth) and find out what pleases the Lord. . . .
But everything exposed by the light becomes visible —
and everything that is illuminated becomes a light.

Ephesians 5:8-10, 13

Growing up, we are barraged by myriad images and lessons about sexuality and womanhood. We learn — through what we see in our families, in our schools, in the media and in our communities — about who we are as girls, and who we are to become as women. But we also learn about sexuality and womanhood through what is *not* talked about. Our sexuality and womanhood are at times shaped just as much by the darkness of fears and the silence of unanswered questions as by the more overt lessons.

These questions are often the reason women seek me out at retreats or at my counseling practice — women like Katie and Jane. Katie is in her early twenties and has masturbated every night for as long as she can remember. Her mom caught her masturbating when she was a little girl and responded with shock and discipline, so she often feels overwhelmed with shame. Katie used to hear boys joking about it and wondered why boys weren't ashamed—and if she is the only girl who does it.

Jane is a forty-one-year-old single woman who is deeply committed in her faith. Recently she disclosed, through tears of shame, that she has always been sexually attracted to women. Despite her intense desire to be "normal," she has never felt physically attracted to a man. She has grown up believing homosexuality is wrong, and she is terrified of what people would do if they knew the truth about her. The weight of Jane's shame and confusion has become suffocating, and she has even found herself thinking about suicide as a way to escape her pain.

MYTH: SEXUALITY SHOULD NOT BE TALKED ABOUT

As Christian women seeking to reflect God's love and character in our lives and relationships, how do we respond to questions and experiences like these? Although it may be tempting to turn away and ignore the confusing and sometimes uncomfortable questions, we cannot and must not respond with silence. Fear and shame are bred in silence, whereas love lives in the light. Therefore, we need to stand with confidence in God's presence in the light of his love, trusting that God can handle any of our questions. Our darkness and shame do not and cannot overshadow God's redemptive love for us. We need to live as children of the light and find out what pleases the Lord—rather than run away from the questions and live in the darkness of sin or fear or shame.

Even when we desire to bring our questions and struggles into the light, we may feel lost, without a map, trying to navigate a murky terrain. If we go to a Bible concordance and look up *pornography* or *masturbation*, what do we find? Not much. This does not mean God is silent on these topics, but it does mean we can't cut and paste Bible verses to give as pat, simplistic answers to questions that are often born out of confusion and pain.

In my work as a psychologist, I am often asked about taboo topics related to sexuality. My husband is also a psychologist, and he specializes in men's sexuality. The two of us love doing retreats and conferences on marriage, sex and gender. We always utilize a question box and give participants cards to write anonymous questions. Regardless of the setting and the population, whether we are speaking with college students or adults, males or females, singles or married folks, several consistent themes emerge in the questions. The five most common questions center around issues related to masturbation, sexual activity before marriage, sexual orientation, sexual addiction and sexual behavior (experimentation) within marriage. For the remainder of this chapter, I will explore the first three questions. Sexual behavior within marriage and sexual addiction will be examined in the next chapter.

Each of these questions could merit an entire chapter or book on its own, and it would be impossible to provide a complete answer to each question—so I will not attempt to do that. Instead, I will walk through how my husband and I approach the questions themselves: we pray with grace and humility. For each of these complex questions, I will rely heavily on the guiding principle that *sexuality should always make us more human, not less.* To be human is to be made in God's image, reflecting God's love, unity and difference in our relationships. Our sexuality should never be dehumanizing; instead, it should allow us to reflect the truth of God's character and love in unique ways. Throughout this section, I will encourage you to look for ways you can reflect God more clearly in your sexual behavior and relationships.

IS MASTURBATION WRONG?

Masturbation is one of the most taboo topics among Christian women. Many women associate masturbation with shame, perhaps because it was never discussed openly with adults or peers as a young or teenage girl. Alternately, some women equate masturbation with the hypersexuality of popular culture discussed in the last chapter. In other words, masturbation is for the kind of women on MTV or *Girls Gone Wild*.

When Katie disclosed her struggle with masturbation in a reflection paper for one of my classes on female sexuality, she said, "I don't ever talk about this, because I really feel like I'm the only one who does it. If the topic is brought up somehow, I hear girls call it 'gross' or make faces. But then I don't understand why guys joke about it so openly, and no one seems to think it's gross or strange for them. I've tried to stop for years, but I never seem to have success. Having some accountability would probably help, but I don't have that because I can't admit that I do it to anyone." Katie is a committed Christian who feels very alone in her struggle, with a multitude of unanswered questions about masturbation, both regarding its sinfulness and the cultural double standard on gender and masturbation.

Katie's questions about masturbation, however, need to be explored *not* through the lens of popular culture or childhood shame but in light of God's character and who he calls us to be—that is, people who reflect his light and love in our personhood and relationships. Masturbation, by definition, goes against the purpose of sex, which is to draw us into union with another person. Sex is meant to be an exchange where each person gives to the other what the other cannot give themselves. Masturbation is a direct effort to give ourselves a gift that is meant to be given to us by another. Masturbation also feeds into the myth that sexual behavior is ultimately a goal-oriented activity culminating in orgasm. Sex should really be about union, not orgasm.

Masturbation is also problematic when it is compulsive or accompanied by unhealthy thoughts or behaviors (e.g., pornography or lustful fantasies about inappropriate people). Sexuality should be always urging us toward union with God and others; if it dehumanizes others or leads us to withdraw from others, this takes away from God's intended purposes. When masturbation is used as a replacement for sexual intimacy with one's spouse (rather than to increase intimacy with one's spouse), this again defeats the purpose of sexuality. Masturbation, however, may not always be harmful. For single women, it can provide a substitute (albeit, ultimately, an unfulfilling one) for sexual behavior outside of marriage. Almost half of teenagers will be sexually active before the end of high school.[1] For those single women who attempt to go against the tide of exploring one's sexuality with a partner, masturbation can provide a release for genuine sexual feelings. Often, women are taught to turn themselves off sexually before marriage—with the expectation that, once married, they will immediately be completely comfortable and uninhibited. Masturbation offers an alternative to this black-and-white view of sexuality; it can be a way of being sexual in one's body as a single person, confirming the reality that all of us are sexual beings—not simply those who are married.

For married women, masturbation can be used to increase pleasure and intimacy within marriage. When women have difficulty with orgasm, for example, it is often due in part to a lack of knowledge about how their bodies work physiologically. The self-exploration of masturbation can ultimately increase connection with a spouse and be an intimacy strengthener.

In a perfect world, masturbation would probably not exist. It is a substitute for the real thing. But the truth is that sex itself is a substitute for the real thing: ultimate union with Christ. Sociologist Lisa McMinn describes masturbation this way: "When we understand that we are made for relationship, that we are existentially alone in our embodied state, yearning for a powerful connection that is fundamentally expressed in our sexuality, then we see masturbation as an attempt to fulfill a longing for intimacy. As a substitute, it is poor and sad, but masturbating represents a longing that is good."[2]

If masturbation controls our lives or leads to other sinful behaviors, then it is like any addiction that needs to be addressed. But as we journey through a broken world in broken bodies and with broken relationships, masturbation may not be the black-and-white evil that many of us learned as young girls.

HOW FAR CAN I GO (SEXUALLY) BEFORE MARRIAGE?

When I was in college, I developed a ritual for getting through the stress of final exams, term papers and so on: I made lists. I would begin making lists whenever I felt that familiar knot in my stomach, warning me that I might not get everything done. Included in my lists were all tasks that needed to be accomplished, even those I did without thinking, like taking a shower or going to class. Like list-makers everywhere, I enjoyed the feeling of accomplishment as I checked off completed items, and it also helped me plan my time. I know that I am not alone in this, and I continue to use list making as a stress-management technique. When I start to feel overwhelmed or out of control, having clear rules (and maybe even lists!) can provide comforting structure and boundaries.

When single folks ask how far they can go sexually, it reminds me of my lists. It is an effort to gain a sense of control over an area that can feel overwhelming. The question is thoughtful and wise, because it acknowledges the power of sexuality. At times, sexual desire can feel like the ocean at high tide, pulling us out into deep water. Although heading into that water may not be the safest or smartest thing to do, its appeal is great.

Implicit in this question is an assumption we share: physical sexual union is reserved for marriage. As Lauren Winner writes, sex outside of marriage "is a wrong reflection of a right creational impulse. We were made for sex. And so premarital sex tells a partial truth; that's why it resonates with something. But partial truths are destructive. They push us to created goods wrongly lived."[3] Sexual desire is powerful, because it was created by God, and it is good.

This question about sexual behavior before marriage is complicated. First, a question asking about sexual behavior *before* marriage assumes that marriage is guaranteed. The truth is that many single folks will not get married or will be single again. This question also reflects an inaccurate rhetoric that marriage is the goal for all individuals: "The expectation that genital sexuality is the reward for earlier abstinence reinforces the idea that marriage ultimately fulfills all longings and that singleness is a sign of failure to find love. Sexuality is expressed in personhood, apart from whether or not people eventually marry."[4] Rather than focusing simply on sexual behavior before marriage, we will explore the importance of boundaries around sexual behavior that takes place outside the confines of marriage.

Perhaps you are single and in a dating relationship. You are attracted to your significant other and drawn to him emotionally and physically. Questions about sexual behavior and intimacy are normal. But instead of asking, "How far can I go?" perhaps a better question is, "What kind of sexual behavior is fitting, life giving, and reflective of God's love and light in my life and relationship with this person right now?" I have heard many Christian authors and speakers suggest very specific boundaries regarding sexual behavior, such as

- no kissing is allowed (holding hands and hugging are okay)
- kissing is allowed but for time-limited periods
- kissing is allowed but no sexual touch (i.e., no touching of any body parts typically covered by a bathing suit) nor mutual masturbation (body contact that leads to orgasm)

Certainly following any of these structures could be beneficial for living out one's sexuality in light of who we are as children of God. In practice, however, I find that many Christian folks either feel unable or unwilling to follow these kinds of boundaries. Some see them as unrealistic and antiquated; others see them as good but unattainable. The reality is that most unmarried folks who are attempting to reserve sexual intimacy for marriage follow a much more vague boundary that looks something like this:

- anything but sex (no kind of intercourse allowed)
- anything but genital intercourse (oral and anal intercourse allowed)

All of these attempts to manage the realities of sexual desire have strengths and weaknesses, and I would suggest that a one-size-fits-all boundary is not the best. When considering your own sexual boundaries, it is prudent to reflect on things like your personal sexual experience and history, your particular level of attunement to physical desire, and the difficulty or ease with which you are able to step back from physical intimacy.

It also makes sense to consider the level of intimacy and commitment in your relationship. In other words, the physical touch between two sixteen-year-olds on a first date should probably not look the same as the physical touch between an engaged couple in their thirties. Having a list of sexual behavior "dos and don'ts" is not the answer, but intentionally reflecting on how you can more authentically reflect God in your most intimate relationships, and then committing to that in writing and in community with others—that comes much closer.

IS HOMOSEXUALITY WRONG?

When Jane first disclosed her lifelong same-sex attraction in my counseling office, her pain was palpable. With tears streaming down her cheeks, she described years of self-loathing, shame and guilt. Although she had never acted on her attraction, she had known she was "different" from a very young age. Despite hours of pleading for God to remove her feelings and change her heart, she could not find any relief. In a moment of raw honesty, she exclaimed, "I feel like God made me a total freak." Jane truly believed that God did not and could not love her, and we spent many hours examining the roots of that belief—as well as finding ways to see and stand in the ocean of God's love. Jane's words provide a stark reminder that this is not a simple question, and there are no easy answers to it. Jane and countless others have spent their lives in this question, and I will not belittle that reality with a few pat answers. Rather, I will invite you to *live in* the questions with women like Jane.

One of the challenges is that this question is embedded in a culture where homosexuality is viewed as a politically charged topic that divides communities, churches and families. This kind of thinking turns people into "issues" and reduces people to only their sexual behavior. As Christian anthropologist Jenell Paris writes, "Christians often become absorbed in either affirming or negating the morality of same-sex sex . . . without more complex dialogue about human sexuality and Christian discipleship."[5] My hope is that, in this section, I can do just that—engage in complex dialogue about human sexuality without reducing it to simplistic answers. If you are looking for a simple yes or no answer to this question, then you will likely be disappointed by my response.

Folks in the evangelical Christian community often fixate on the question of whether or not homosexuality is a sin. Many of us have grown up in families and churches where homosexuality was denounced as an abomination, yet we live in the midst of a popular culture that portrays gay individuals as perfectly normal, healthy folks. Some of us may be dealing with our own feelings of same-sex attraction and are afraid to speak up. We may have been taught that people become homosexual because of childhood sexual abuse or other traumatic experiences; we don't know how to reconcile that teaching with a gay friend who has had a healthy upbringing, has no abuse history, and has a loving and supportive family. Or, for those experiencing same-sex attraction, those stereotypes may differ greatly from our personal experience. This was certainly the case for Jane who had a close and loving relationship with both parents and no history of abuse.

In the political rhetoric around sexual orientation, we may have heard that individuals make a choice to live the gay "lifestyle," and yet we have witnessed the real suffering of a dear friend who has desperately tried to choose anything other than homosexuality. Perhaps she is like Jane and has always and only felt attraction for women; consequently, she has suffered with years of depression and self-hatred because of her inability to rid herself of the same-sex attraction. Many loving and compassionate people with a deep faith in God struggle to make sense of what they learned growing up in the church about homosexuality because of exposure to real people like Jane. This is a good thing. When you find out that your daughter or your sister or your best friend is gay, suddenly the Christian catch-phrases about homosexuality sound a little different—a little more angry, mean or hurtful.

As believers in Jesus, it behooves us to seek the wisdom of biblical teaching on sexuality in general and homosexuality in particular. The traditional Christian interpretation of Scripture is that homosexual behavior is wrong. Most folks are familiar with this response, in which several Bible verses are used to denounce homosexuality. Often these arguments are followed up with an exhortation to have compassion on homosexual people without condoning their behavior. We have all heard the adage that we should "hate the sin but love the sinner." In other words, we should love homosexual people, even if we do not love their behavior.

Although this sounds good, because we all sin and are all in need of forgiveness and grace, let's take a good, honest look at our evangelical churches. Are there people in our churches who lie, covet, or have addictions to pornography and alcohol? Are there folks who are having sex outside of marriage? Those kinds of sinners have sat next to me (a fellow sinner) at every church I've been in, yet how many gay men or lesbians are sitting next to us in church? Is it possible that we in the evangelical church are not very successful at loving the sinner—when the sinner is gay? Our churches are filled with folks committing any number of sins, but for some reason, most gay and lesbian individuals are not filling the pews of our churches.

Jane spoke to that reality in a recent conversation with me. She is celibate, is deeply committed to her faith and involved in her church, but she recently told me that if anyone knew of her same-sex attraction, she would have to leave her church. "They would never look at me the same or treat me the same. I couldn't handle that." Philip Yancey quotes a gay man's reflections on this reality in more blunt terms: "As a gay man, I've found it's easier for me to get sex on the streets than to get a hug in church."[6] Perhaps this is because, as Jenell Paris suggests, many evangelicals not only treat homosexuality as a sin, but as a separate and worse offense than others: "For many Christians, homosexuality pads the bottom of the sin barrel, so no matter how low a heterosexual may go, at least she or he hasn't gone as low as *them*."[7]

In contrast to the traditional Christian answer, gay-affirming Christians argue that homosexuality is not wrong. They suggest that the Bible is silent on sexual orientation as we know it today, and it does not speak to the possibility of a committed same-sex relationship. Rather, the Bible speaks with judgment on a number of homosexual acts that involved prostitutes or other kinds of accompanying offenses, such as an attack on hospitality. Gay-affirming Christians also point out the importance of the cultural context of the biblical writings, saying we live in a different world. While we constantly make judgments about what specific behavioral mandates in the Bible are applicable for today, they say that those judgments are simply that— our own judgments and interpretations. For example, most folks don't believe women need to cover their heads or sit in a separate part of the church, even though those things are prescribed biblically. However, most contemporary believers would say that those kinds of behavioral restrictions are not necessary or relevant for

today, and gay-affirming folks apply that same logic to the verses in
the Bible related to homosexual behavior.

Perhaps you have heard arguments on both sides of the morality
of same-sex orientation and still feel unsure. My friend Anne has a
daughter who is a deeply committed Christian—and she is also a
lesbian. Anne recently told me, "I don't know how to make sense of
it—gay or straight—but if I'm going to err on one side or the other, I
want to err on love. I want to love my daughter well." Her words
brought tears to my eyes and resonated deep within me. For many
religious people, homosexuality is a big "issue," but to speak of homosexuality as an issue is to tell a false story. Sexuality—whether gay
or straight—is about people, people who are created in the image of
God and reflect that image in beautiful and broken ways—just like
all of us.

Recently I was talking with Jane about the journey she has been
on over the last year. When she first disclosed her same-sex attraction,
she had a long-term history of withdrawing from friendships as they
became closer. She hid herself in many ways from all those around
her. Over time, she has begun to engage in more authentic ways with
those in her community. Jane is still celibate but is no longer sure
what she believes about the morality of homosexual behavior; she has
begun to feel more at peace with herself. I reflected this change and
equated it with her ability to be more honest with herself and others.
She disagreed vehemently and stated, "No, while I am different, it's
because for the first time I really believe that God loves me. Not
people in general, but *me*." I hope we can all follow Jane's lead and
remember that our identity begins and ends not with externals such
as single or married, parent or childless, gay or straight, but with this
truth: we are beloved children of God.

For those of us who have grown up in the evangelical subculture,
masturbation, sexual behavior outside of marriage, and same-sex attraction are often cloaked in shame and fear. In order to experience

the sexual wholeness that God offers, we can and should bring all of ourselves into the light of his presence. We can invite God into every corner of our being, asking him to breathe life and light into us. We are sexual beings who can reflect God's love in our thoughts, feelings and behaviors, but we are not perfect. We will struggle with sexual sin, whether we are young or old, married or single. But that struggle need not be in silence. Instead, we can pursue wisdom and accountability with other Christ-followers in community as we seek to live out our lives as sexual beings.

6

Sex, Power and
Fifty Shades of Grey

I am free to make choices about what I do and do not do.
But pay attention to this: Those choices should be made
in light of who I am, not to determine who I am. I am one
in whom Christ dwells, and that should guide my decisions.
Will this activity be beneficial to me? Will that activity
enslave me? . . . Understanding our true identity and
acting from that is a much stronger motivator than guilt.

James Bryan Smith,
The Good and Beautiful God

Sex and power often go together in our culture. Henry Kissinger's famous quote, "Power is the ultimate aphrodisiac"[1] finds support in political sex scandals (Bill Clinton, Eliot Spitzer, Anthony Weiner or John Ensign, just to name a few) and popular culture. In 2011, the female author E. L. James released *Fifty Shades of Grey*, the now-infamous romance novel that eroticizes the sex-power connection.

For many people, *Fifty Shades of Grey* is synonymous with graphic sex scenes and the practice of bondage/discipline and sadism/

masochism. Sometimes referred to as "mommy porn," James's book has sold over 70 million copies and is the fastest-selling paperback of all time (surpassing *Harry Potter*). The book caused quite a stir, and some women were intense critics—of its hypersexuality, pornographic nature or degrading acts toward women. The Internet was flooded with blogs and Facebook posts from women who were disturbed by the book and urged people to boycott it. The vast popularity of the book, however, tells us that a large majority of women bought into *Fifty Shades of Grey*.

But long before *Fifty Shades* came out, popular culture has been telling a story of anything-goes sexuality. If we believe what we see in the movies, on TV and in romance novels, then we can do whatever we want sexually, with whomever we want, whenever we want. We can have as many partners as we want, as long as we practice safe sex. We can consume whatever sexual material we want as long as we are not hurting anyone. Nothing is off-limits. Many Christians have challenged the morality of this sexual ethic, and rightly so. But how do we respond to questions about sexual morality and behavior without reducing them to oversimplified answers? In this chapter the relationship between sex and power will be explored, specifically as it applies to sexual experimentation within marriage and sexually addictive behaviors.

MYTH: SEX IS POWER

What messages are women ingesting when they consume books like *Fifty Shades of Grey*? Consider the basic plotline: The main character is Ana, a beautiful twenty-one-year-old college student who is unsure of herself and seems unaware of her own beauty. She is a virgin until she meets the protagonist of the novel, Christian. He is a handsome twenty-seven-year-old billionaire who asks Ana to sign a contract agreeing to be his sexual submissive. Ana's character is a personification of the Madonna-whore archetype, while Christian is clearly a troubled soul in need of rescue. Christian feels powerful when dominating women sexually. In fact, when Ana willingly loses her virginity to Christian the scene sounds more like rape than anything else. She states that he "rips through my virginity" and then looks down at her, "his eyes bright with ecstatic triumph."[2] For Christian, sex is about overt displays and experiences of power—winning, victory and domination. For Ana, sex is about a covert kind of power, as she learns to use her own sexual appeal to influence and ultimately tame Christian into what she wants.

Men who are powerful have long been using women for sex, and women have been using sex to attain power from men since the beginning of time. *Fifty Shades of Grey* is not breaking any new ground here, although the explicit use of violence adds a disturbing and problematic association. Not only does the man use the woman for sex, he associates her pain with his own sexual arousal. When we connect physiological sexual arousal with violent images or experiences, we forge neural pathways that ask to be repeated. This is the foundation of sexual violence, and it is frightening and perplexing to observe how millions of women have been willing to learn this lesson. If men feel powerful by sexualizing women, then women seem to be following suit—sexualizing, objectifying, degrading and demeaning women as well.

In this chapter, the relationship between sex and power will be examined as it specifically relates to the last two questions my husband, Jeff, and I get asked most often: about sexual experimentation in marriage and sexual addiction. One of the things I have always been drawn to in Jeff is his ability to sit with painful questions and be a vessel of God's healing presence without offering quick fixes or easy answers. I have asked Jeff to join me in this chapter, particularly to share his expertise in the area of sexual addiction and to help me respond to the complexities involved in the stories of women like Leslie and Emma.

Leslie is a thirty-year-old, newly married woman whose husband pushed her to read *Fifty Shades of Grey* because he thought it would help her become more sexually adventurous. She and her husband dated for many years before getting married, and the longer they have been together, the more her husband has pushed for new sexual behaviors to spice things up. When they were dating, this led to greater and greater physical intimacy and ultimately to a regular sexual relationship before marriage. Now that they are married, her husband is pushing her to experiment with other sexual behaviors.

Emma, on the other hand, is married to a man who was recently fired from his job for looking at pornography at work. Some of her girlfriends immediately labeled him a "sex addict" and counseled her to divorce him. Other friends brushed it off and disclosed that their boyfriends or husbands look at porn sometimes too. Emma is overwhelmed and confused by her situation and her friends' responses. But both Leslie and Emma are struggling to make sense of what healthy sexuality looks like, and how they can grow toward healing and wholeness in their relationships.

IS SEXUAL EXPERIMENTATION WITHIN MARRIAGE OKAY?

Judy grew up in an extremely conservative home where sex was never talked about. Before she got married, her mother pulled her aside and had the "sex talk" with her for the first time—at age twenty-one. Her mother described sex as something a wife did for her husband to keep him satisfied. Never did her mom mention the possibility that there could be sexual pleasure for the wife. Now Judy and her husband have been married eighteen years and have three teenage children; they have sexual intercourse once or twice a week, always at the husband's request. Judy complies, but the sex is always the same: in the dark in the missionary position.

Recently, Judy's best friend got remarried, and she has been talking openly and often about the creativity and pleasure in her sexual relationship with her new husband. These conversations have left Judy feeling embarrassed and a little angry. She is beginning to wonder if she has missed something all these years with her husband, or if there is something wrong with her or her marriage. Judy and her husband began seeing a marriage counselor, and Judy is beginning to question the rules she has always followed in her sexual relationship with her husband.

Leslie, on the other hand, is questioning the *lack* of rules her husband seems to have for sex in their marriage. Unlike Judy, Leslie and her husband never have sex in the missionary position. Instead, he prefers for her to be faced away from him, and recently, he has been pushing her to try anal sex and domination role-plays. Leslie feels like she is always saying no and putting the brakes on their sexual relationship, and she wonders if he has any boundaries around what they can or should do in the bedroom.

Leslie has begun to dread when her husband approaches her sexually, because she doesn't want him to be angry or hurt if she doesn't want to do something he suggests. Leslie acknowledges that she is curious about some of the things her husband wants to do, but she is also afraid of the pain in certain acts. On a deeper level, Leslie worries about her husband's seeming inability to be sexually satisfied with "just me." Leslie doesn't want her husband to think she is prudish or uninterested in sexual intimacy, but she wants to feel safe in their sexual relationship.

Neither Judy nor Leslie feel like their sexual relationships are accurately reflecting God's loving, relational nature. In 1 Corinthians 10:23-24, Paul tells us that while we may have the right to do anything, not everything is beneficial. Instead of seeking our own rights, we need to put others first: "No one should seek their own good, but the good of others." When considering sexual experimentation within marriage, I encourage couples to shift the focus from what is merely acceptable to what brings good to the other. If my husband, for example, is going to reflect God's love in our marriage, then he will be *for* me—seeking my good in all things. Likewise, I will be *for* him. Being *for* me means that Jeff wants me to experience physical pleasure and joy in our sexual relationship, without degrading or hurting me in any way.

If you are wondering about sexual experimentation in your marriage, I would encourage you to ask whether the sexual behavior in question is for the good of the other. The answer is not only in the act itself but in the relationship and intimacy between the partners. For example, for a woman who was sexually abused by an uncle who forced her to perform oral sex, that particular sexual act may be something that she cannot do without feeling violated. Oral sex is not innately wrong, but if her husband tries to pressure her into it because of his own desire, that would be seeking his own good instead of the good of his wife.

When asking questions about sexual behavior in marriage, I encourage couples to take time to reflect on the relationship and intimacy level. What are you hoping to get more of in the marriage through the sexual behavior? Are you looking for greater intimacy as a couple, or is it only about getting a better orgasm for yourself? Pleasure is a God-created gift, but the pursuit of pleasure at the cost of your spouse may be less than loving. Sometimes the most loving thing you can do is to *receive* pleasure from your spouse. Pleasure and orgasm are not wrong, but a deeper reflection on the motivation for sexual experimentation can help clarify the potential impact on the relationship. In addition, I ask couples to consider some general questions about the specific sexual behavior they are considering:

- Is this sexual behavior going to foster a kind of intimacy with something or someone other than your spouse (versus strengthening face-to-face intimacy with your spouse)?
- Is anyone going to be physically or emotionally hurt by this behavior?
- Will either partner be demeaned and depersonalized in any way?

Sexuality should always make us more human, not less so, and just because something is done in the context of marriage does not automatically make it holy and life-giving. The problem with sadism/masochism is that "the movement is not toward, but away from, responsible loving and caring. The focus is upon the pain rather than the building of a relationship."[3] Marriage is about intimacy and the pursuit of another's good. Sex within marriage is a good and beautiful thing created by God to reflect his love for us—and his future union with us. Our job is to enact the truth of what sex is with what we actually do in our own bodies and relationships.

WHAT IS SEXUAL ADDICTION?

James is a forty-five-year-old man who recently lost his job after it was discovered that he had been consistently looking at pornography in the workplace. His wife of twenty years, Emma, was shocked and embarrassed by James's behavior and its consequences. Although they began seeing a marriage counselor, Emma asked James for a separation while she contemplated whether she could stay in the marriage. James stopped attending church because of his own shame, and because his wife was not comfortable with the family worshiping together since they were separated. James has a sexual addiction, which has left a devastating wake on his family. James lost his job, damaged his marital relationship, and found himself estranged from his church.

Unfortunately, while sexual addiction is a topic that is getting greater attention in the media and the church in recent years, it is certainly not a new phenomenon. In fact, many would argue that the story of David and Bathsheba paints a picture of a man with a sex addiction. David, the man after God's own heart, was so intent on possessing Bathsheba that he ignored social and moral rules that would prohibit him from having her. His pursuit sounds less about loving some*one* than wanting to have some*thing*. This desire to consume or have is consistent with a sexual addiction. As Kent Dunnington writes, "Addiction simplifies and orders life by narrowing the focus of the addicted person onto one object, one 'final end.'"[4] Despite its ancient presence, the current cultural climate provides ample opportunity for anyone struggling with sexually addictive behavior. Our senses are flooded with distortions of sexuality every day.

Many individuals, both men and women, struggle with sexual purity at various points in their lives. For one woman, it might be an occasional glance at an attractive man (who is not her husband) that lasts a bit too long. For another, it might be reading and fantasizing about the contents of a sexually explicit book series. For yet another, it might be a few minutes of Internet pornography sporadically throughout the year. Many of us engage in sexual thoughts or behaviors that are outside a biblical picture of holiness. But regardless of whether individual behaviors are sinful or healthy, isolated incidents of sexually questionable behavior are not the same as a sexual addiction. In other words, all people who struggle with sexual impurity are not sex addicts.

Sexual addiction has less to do with the nature of the sexual stimuli being consumed than with the purpose behind the consumption. The sexual material could be anything from looking at celebrity photos on Internet photo galleries to seeking out prostitutes on business trips. Those who *chronically* seek material for sexual arousal as an *escape from reality* or as a *substitute for intimacy* are operating in an addictive fashion. Often, individuals struggling with a sex addiction deny or minimize the severity of their behavior. When a person's sexual behavior is out of control and has negative consequences, he or she could likely be diagnosed with a sexual addiction.

Sexual addiction is not something that happens only to men, though it does occur more frequently among men. Because of its greater prevalence among men, many women who are interested in understanding sexual addiction do so because of their husband's behavior—or a friend's husband's actions. Women can also become sexually addicted (see appendix for resources, especially Marnie Ferree's 2010 book, *No Stones*), but I will use masculine language for the remainder of this chapter to reflect the more common experience.

We are often asked why a man would sacrifice his family for an unreal fantasy on a computer screen, or why politicians risk their careers for sexually inappropriate communication, or how men can pay for sex with women and girls in the sex trade. In a marital session with a man suffering from sex addiction, the wife of one of Jeff's clients said to him, "I just don't understand why my husband would give up his family for a picture in a box." No single answer can provide a universal explanation for compulsive sex-seeking behavior, although Betty Friedan argued that "compulsive sexual activity, homosexual or heterosexual, usually veils a lack of potency in other spheres of life."[5]

On the other hand, some blame sexually compulsive behavior on men's high levels of testosterone, which are approximately 40-60 times stronger in adult men than women. And neuroscientist William Struthers, in his book *Wired for Intimacy: How Pornography Hijacks the Male Brain*, describes a step-by-step neurological framework that can lead to sexually addictive behavior:

> This is how a pornography addiction and sexual compulsion is built from scratch. It involves the visual system (looking at porn), the motor system (masturbating), the sensory system (genital stimulation) and neurological effects of orgasm (sexual euphoria from opiates, addictive dopamine in the nucleus accumbens and reduced fear in the amygdale). They have now begun to store this pattern as a reinforced neurological habit.[6]

Like Struthers's model suggests, James's consumption of pornography did not begin all at once; it developed over time. Like many sex addicts, James had found ways to rationalize and justify his behavior: "This is something all guys do," he told himself. "It's not really a big deal." What began as periodic perusals of his wife's bathing suit catalogs had progressed to daily consumption of hardcore pornography in the workplace. As he continued to act on these impulses, James found he needed to engage in riskier behavior and more distorted pornography to achieve the same level of satisfaction. As Rob Bell points out, "Lust does not operate on a flat line, as if we can give in and stay at the same level of consumption indefinitely. . . . Lust always wants more."[7] In the moment, all James cared about was consuming more sexual material, and the impact on the bigger picture of life was far from his thought process.

Sexual addiction is about more than sex. It is also about a desire to be in control, to have power and to possess. All three of these things drive us to act out in numerous ways in our lives. When we feel unsettled and out of control, we look for things to help us feel better. Engaging in sexual sin is one way to try to fill the void, albeit in a manner that leads to a deeper sense of emptiness. James was seeking to fill a space left by broken relationships in his past and had an inability to forge real intimacy in his marriage, but the sexual behavior he found was ultimately empty and unfulfilling.

If someone truly has a sexual addiction, what can he or she do to get better? Because sexuality emanates from the core of who we are, addressing sexual addiction is a challenging process. In the disease model, sexual addiction is treated as an illness similar to alcohol or drug addiction. In the sin model, the sexually addictive behavior is viewed strictly as an issue of sin in the individual's life, and the behavior is treated as any other sin that needs to be rooted out through prayer and submission to Christ. *Alternately*, an integrative approach synthesizes the spiritual and disease models, acknowledging the power and hold of addiction on an individual's life, while also addressing the volitional choices to sin that have been involved in the sexual behavior.

James participated in a treatment program that incorporated both the disease and sin models. He met with an individual therapist, as well as a group of men for accountability. In his group, he was challenged to honestly disclose his own sin, as well as to challenge and encourage the other men in his group. This combination—understanding the roots of his behavior in past hurts and dealing with the challenge to relate to other men in an accountability community—provided a path to healing.

Emma and James continued to work with a marriage counselor while James was pursuing his own treatment. The marriage counselor emphasized the importance of Emma giving herself permission to be angry and to express that anger to James directly. At the same time, like so many who struggle with addiction, James was mired in a world of shame and guilt, and he at times felt truly powerless to live in a different way. While Emma needed to respond with challenge or confrontation as a result of being hurt by her husband's sexual sin, she also found ways to reach out and love her repentant spouse. Emma set clear boundaries with James to protect herself and their marriage, asserting that she would not sit by and allow herself to continue to be sinned against as they moved forward.

If sexual addiction is about consumption, then healing is about intimacy. Addiction leads people to value possession and consumption of sexual stimuli over anything else. God calls us to pursue intimacy with God and others over all things. No single approach to recovery from sexual addiction is perfect, but the antidote to addiction is intimacy—the intentional pursuit of intimacy with God, spouse and a community of fellow travelers on the journey toward sexual wholeness.

A NEW KIND OF POWER

Our culture tells us that sex and power go hand in hand. Power allows us to pursue and consume sex or sexual stimuli at our own discretion and for our own pleasure. Jesus offers a different lesson about power, and when we take seriously the call to model our lives after Christ, then we will see power through a different lens. Jesus did not use power to hurt, control, manipulate, coerce, degrade or harm others. Instead, he used his power to serve and love: "Jesus used his power to lift up the fallen, to forgive the guilty, to encourage maturity in the weak. Most notably, he honored those who occupied a marginal status (women and children) in the patriarchal culture of New Testament times. He was an empowerer of people."[8] While the movies, books and political scandals of our day may suggest that sex is power, we know a different truth: love is power. Power is being *for* another person. Living out God's self-giving love in authentic relationship with others is power.

As James Bryan Smith suggests in this chapter's epigraph, our choices "should be made in light of who I am, not to determine who I am."[9] Our sexual-behavior choices should not be about getting or maintaining power. Rather, they should be made in light of the reality that we are beloved creatures made in God's image, designed to reflect God's character in our lives and relationships. Ideally, our choices do not make us; we make choices because of who we are as children of God. We can use our power not to sexualize or be sexualized, but to join Christ in loving others and being for them.

7

Healing from Unwanted Sexual Experiences

there is a part of me that is in continual pain.
sometimes i walk through a crowd of people
barely able to keep my composure. i still cry myself
to sleep. my sadness is sometimes bottomless;
it won't let me meet my own eyes in the mirror.

Renee Altson,
Stumbling Toward Faith

I recently took a weekend trip, alone with my husband, back to my home state for a high-school reunion. While there, we also spent some time in Ann Arbor, Michigan, where I went to college. It had been several years since I had been on the campus, and I loved taking Jeff around town to my favorite coffee shops and bookstores. I was dismayed, however, by another set of memories that flooded me during this nostalgic trip. As we passed my freshman dorm, a local fraternity house and an ex-boyfriend's apartment building, I was reminded of some of my own unwanted sexual experiences. I was thankful for my husband's gentleness and grace as we talked through some very shame-filled moments of my college years.

In this chapter, we will take a closer look at the relationship between shame and sexuality. As we have discussed throughout this book, sexuality is central to how God has created us in his image. It makes sense, then, that when we experience sexual wounds, those wounds run deep. When our sexuality is violated, it affects us to our core. Trauma of any sort, such as physical violence, emotional abuse or neglect, impacts us deeply. For the purposes of this chapter, however, we will focus on two common sources of sexual wounds: sexual abuse and unwanted sexual experiences.

Jaime is a fifty-year-old woman who was sexually abused by her uncle for several years, beginning when she was ten years old. What began as affectionate touch eventually turned into sexual touch and intercourse. Jaime loved her uncle as a little girl, and she was confused by the emotional and physical feelings this created. Every aspect of Jaime's beliefs about herself and about sex have been filtered through her childhood sexual abuse.

Meanwhile, Katelyn is a nineteen-year-old young woman who has felt repeatedly pushed into sexual encounters that she did not want. Her most recent experience was at the end of a date; after a period of kissing in her date's car, he suddenly unzipped his pants and pushed her head down toward his genitals. Katelyn tried to resist, but eventually she complied: "I felt like it was my fault—that I'd put myself in the situation. And I just wanted it to end so I could get out of there."

MYTH: WHAT YOU HAVE DONE (OR HAD DONE TO YOU) IS WHO YOU ARE

Jaime and Katelyn have both experienced sexual wounds. In this chapter I will explore how God can and does offer restoration to each of us. Because abuse affects us so deeply, healing requires a holistic examination of the impact on our body, mind, behavior and social identity. Who we are is not what we have done or had done to us sexually; rather, who we are is who we are becoming in Christ. Healing from sexual abuse and trauma is an extensive process, and this chapter is not intended to be exhaustive. Rather, it is an introduction to some pathways to healing for both sexual abuse and unwanted sexual experiences.[1]

Talking about sexual wounds is painful business. It may be tempting to skip some of these sections—perhaps because it may not seem applicable to your own experience or because the discussion is, by nature, somewhat explicit or feels distressing. Let me encourage you to persist, even if and when it becomes uncomfortable. The unfortunate reality is that women who are sexually abused are not a small minority. Estimates vary, but it is suggested that anywhere between 20-40 percent of females experience sexual abuse at some point in their childhood.[2] Estimates on women experiencing unwanted sexual experiences in adolescence and adulthood are even higher. The likelihood that you or someone you love has experienced sexual abuse or unwanted sexual experiences is very high.

Being able to sit in the light of God's truth of love and redemption also means that we must be willing and able to sit in the darkness of others' and our own real experiences of pain, shame and despair. Hope and light do not appear by waving a magic wand; rather they are born through what is often painful work and also in safe, reparative, healing relationships. In this chapter, we will explore the healing journey from shame to hope.

THE WOUND OF SEXUAL ABUSE

Jaime, the woman whose uncle forced her to have sexual intercourse with him, is clearly the victim of childhood sexual abuse. But what about Leslie, who woke up on a family camping trip to find her older cousin watching her and masturbating? Or Christina, whose grandfather would have her sit on his lap and rub her thighs while he had an erection? Both Leslie and Christina felt ashamed and embarrassed about these experiences, but they also wrote them off, telling themselves, "He was just a dirty old man," or "he was raging with hormones." So what exactly *is* sexual abuse?

Sexual abuse is defined as any and all sexual activity between an adult and a child, or between children when there is a significant difference in age (usually three or more years), size or power.[3] Sexual abuse may involve physical contact, in which a child is forced to participate in behavior that the adult is using for his or her own sexual stimulation. Specific examples might include

- fondling or touching of child's sexual body parts, or child touching adult's body parts
- kissing or French-kissing on mouth or body parts
- asking child to sit on the lap of a male with an erection
- masturbation in presence of child, forcing child to masturbate the adult
- penetration of the child with any object or body part
- oral, anal or vaginal sex

Sexual abuse can also be classified as noncontact, in which a child is forced to look at or listen to sexually explicit material, or if a child is forced to be looked at sexually without physical touch. Specific examples might include

- showing a child pornography in any form (video, magazine or Internet)
- an adult exposing his or her sexual body parts to the child
- forcing a child to listen to sexual comments about herself or others
- looking at a child without his or her clothes on
- taking sexualized pictures of a child

By definition, Jaime, Leslie and Christina all experienced sexually abusive behavior, and they are not alone. As mentioned above, most researchers estimate that between one in three and one in four women are sexually abused in childhood at some point.[4] This means if your church has 200 women, about fifty or sixty of those women have probably experienced some kind of sexual abuse.

It may be hard to believe that so many women have survived sexual abuse. "I only know one woman in my church who was sexually abused as a child," you may think. Sexual abuse, however, is immersed in secrecy and shame. Just because women do not talk openly about sexual abuse does not mean it does not exist. Women may remain silent because of fear of judgment from others, from fear of stigma, because they blame themselves for the abuse or simply because it is too painful.

THE WOUND OF UNWANTED SEXUAL EXPERIENCES

In addition to the horror of childhood sexual abuse, many adolescent and adult women have had unwanted sexual experiences. Katelyn, the young woman whose date pushed her into having oral sex in his car, is one of many women who has experienced unwanted sexual activity. In one study, 41 percent of teenage girls between the ages of fourteen and seventeen reported having experienced unwanted sex.[5] Over half of the women in numerous studies of college females report unwanted sexual experiences.[6]

For many women, the unwanted sexual experience was sexual intercourse—also known as rape. For others, it may be an unwanted or uninvited sexual touch, kiss or other behavior. Sometimes the unwanted sexual experience is preceded by a clearly voiced "no" from the woman. Other times, women feel as if they cannot say no—because they feel pressured, afraid of the male's response or because of a sense of responsibility. A student in one of sociologist Lisa McMinn's classes described the sexual pressure she felt: "I totally felt like I should please him, and deep down I somehow felt that I owed it to him."[7]

The epidemic level of unwanted sexual experiences among women should be alarming. When I was a resident adviser at a large, state university, I was horrified by the number of conversations I had with eighteen- and nineteen-year-old girls who had been pushed into sexual situations. It was common knowledge that fraternities referred to those first vulnerable days of the school year as (excuse my frank language here) "freshman f*** week."

I could spend quite a long time exploring some of the reasons why this is happening to young women, but instead I want to focus on the healing journey. Regardless of how the unwanted sexual experience happens, when women are unable to use their voices and bodies to choose how and when they want to be sexual, the damage to their emotional and physical well-being can be extensive. Once a woman has experienced this kind of unwanted sexual activity, how does it impact her and how can she heal from those experiences?

SCARS LEFT BEHIND

Sexual abuse and unwanted sexual experiences are traumatic and have been connected with psychological difficulties, such as depression, anxiety, self-harm and addiction. They have also been associated with medical problems and physical complaints.[8] Sexual abuse and unwanted sexual experiences can lead to a number of difficulties with sexual functioning and intimacy, as well as self-image. What follows are a few of the common, negative consequences of abuse.

Self-blame. One of the most common negative effects of sexual abuse is self-blame. Women often believe the abuse was somehow their fault or their responsibility. Many women have difficulty naming it as "abuse" because of these beliefs. Survivors may believe that, in some way, they led the offender to do it, or they blame themselves because they did not resist or because their body responded to the abuse:

She sees herself participating in forbidden sexual activity and may often get some sense of gratification from it even if she doesn't want to (it is, after all, a form of touch, and our bodies respond without the consent of our wills). This is seen as further proof that the abuse is her fault and well deserved. In her mind, she has become responsible for the actions of her abusers. She believes she is not a victim.[9]

Sexual abuse is never the victim's fault. Any sexual contact between an adult and a child is always and only the responsibility of the adult, and it is never okay. As Wendy Maltz writes, "No one is responsible for the abuse except the offender. . . . No matter how you behaved, you had a right not to be sexually abused."[10] For survivors of sexual abuse, learning to believe this truth not only with their minds but also in their hearts and bodies can be monumental.

For women who have experienced unwanted sexual activity, self-blame can be especially confusing. When a woman (or a man) resists in any way, any sexual activity should always stop. When a man continues to push a teenager or woman sexually after she resists in her body or voice, this is violating and wrong.

But what about the woman (*not* child) who did not want to engage in a particular sexual activity, but did not communicate any resistance with her words or behavior? The experience is unwanted, but her lack of consent is unknown to her partner. In these situations, forgiveness of self and exploration of ways to strengthen one's voice are important.

Distorted view of sex. Lauren Winner writes, "Sex can make us feel that we are just bodies, just places where other people thoughtlessly and even anonymously act out their desires."[11] In no case is this more true than when a woman has been violated in her sexuality. Sexual abuse and unwanted sexual experiences are dehumanizing experiences, in which the designed one-flesh intimacy of sexual union is completely dismembered. Instead, the sexual behavior is an act that is done *to* the woman. Consequently, violating sexual experiences can lead to unhealthy views of sex.

Some women who have been sexually violated develop an extremely negative view of sex, associating it with shame, fear or pain. Sex becomes something to be avoided or simply endured. Ultimately, sex is seen as unsafe because it has been used to hurt, control and damage. Regardless of the current context (e.g., in a loving marriage relationship), sex is still experienced this way. Women may experience sexual dysfunctions as adults because of these distorted views of sex, such as difficulty experiencing sexual arousal or orgasm. As sex therapist Doug Rosenau writes, "Abuse victims are sexualized earlier than God intended and in a situation that was the farthest removed from the loving relational experience He designed. Sex becomes associated with fear, pain, and control. The positive feelings of love, joy, and pleasure are absent or distorted."[12]

In contrast to those who develop a very negative view of sex are those women who develop a hypersexual response. For some women, sex becomes a commodity that can be used to attain power or gain control, or they may engage in self-destructive sexual behaviors: "Survivors may compulsively and aggressively seek sexual activities. Believing sex is uncontrollable, survivors may become sexually demanding or may give in to the sexual demands of their partners."[13]

Neither of these responses reflects the truth of what sex is or how God has created us to live in that reality. Sex is a gift, and it is good. It is not a dirty evil to be avoided, nor is it a tool to be used to control or dominate others. Even if it *feels* like that, the truth is that sex *is* good. We are sexual beings, and that is good and beautiful. When the good gift of sex has been distorted into a tool of coercion, violence and power, it can lead to real and long-lasting consequences in later sexual experiences.

Intimacy in relationships. Healthy intimate relationships involve trust, vulnerability and physical touch. All of these things may feel threatening or unsafe to someone who has experienced sexual abuse or unwanted sexual experiences. Because of the betrayal and powerlessness involved in abuse, learning to trust another person can be an arduous task. Exposing one's fears, feelings and thoughts to another may feel downright terrifying.

Individuals who have been sexually violated have often developed a complex pattern of self-protective behaviors. Although these self-protective behaviors may have been adaptive and helpful in the violating environment, they may get in the way of intimate relationships later in life. Learning to discern safe and unsafe people, develop and maintain appropriate boundaries, and foster emotional and physical intimacy in relationships are all essential components of the healing process for the survivor of sexual abuse.

THE HEALING JOURNEY

If you have experienced sexual trauma, I highly encourage you to talk to a trusted friend, mentor, pastor or counselor to assist you in identifying the best path for your own healing journey. Perhaps your journey might include professional counseling, a support group and/ or reading a sexual-abuse recovery book. If you are experiencing suicidal or self-harming thoughts or behaviors, please talk to a loved one and seek professional help immediately. There is hope! Healing is not something that will happen in a vacuum; it happens in the context of relationship and with hard work. The journey is not easy or painless, but I believe it is both necessary and worthwhile in order to experience healing, both with oneself and in relationship with others.

The healing process is an individual one, but for all survivors, healing must be holistic to be effective. Because abuse and unwanted sexual experiences tap into our core personhood, it can affect all parts of us—our bodies, minds, behaviors and social identities. A comprehensive healing journey involves examining all these aspects of selfhood. Here are a few important steps that most of the women survivors I see in counseling engage in as they move toward healing. *Tell your story and allow yourself to grieve.* The healing journey begins with telling your story. Naming the abuse as abuse and the offender as an offender is an important step. The emphasis here is not on blame but on truth.[14] Telling your story means telling the truth about what happened. Sexually violating experiences are shrouded in secrecy. By speaking the truth about what happened to you—to yourself, to a trusted friend or family member, to a counselor, to your spouse—you shed light on darkness.

In Ephesians 5 we are told to expose the fruitless deeds of the darkness: "It is shameful even to mention what the disobedient do in secret. But everything exposed by the light becomes visible—and everything that is illuminated becomes a light" (vv. 12-13). By exposing those deeds to the light, you lessen their power and separate them from the power of secrecy. You also choose to act against the offender's explicit or implicit instructions to keep his or her actions a secret. By telling the truth about what happened, you use your voice in a way you were unable to do when the abuse happened.

The healing process also means allowing yourself to *feel* whatever feelings accompany that story. Perhaps you feel powerlessness, betrayal or anger. These are uncomfortable feelings and the tendency may be to avoid them, numb out or pretend they are not there. But avoidance of true feelings does not help us find healing or redemption. Many women have learned to detach from their emotions in order to protect themselves, but in order to heal, it is important to both speak the truth about what happened and allow yourself to feel.

Sexual abuse and unwanted sexual experiences involve loss. If you experienced sexual trauma, you may feel like you lost a part of yourself in the experience. You may have lost your voice, your innocence, your ability to trust people in general or men in particular. You may have lost aspects of sexual functioning. All of these losses need to be grieved. Some of them can be restored, but before you can heal from loss, it is important to allow yourself to name and grieve those losses. By telling your story, you tell the truth about what happened to your body and your mind (by expressing your real thoughts and feelings).

Identify the impact. As you tell your story, the unique impact those experiences have had on your own self-image, thoughts, feelings and behaviors will become more clear. Perhaps as you tell your story you realize that you labeled yourself a particular way after the abuse, such as "I am a slut." That label, coupled with your experiences, may have then impacted the sexual choices you made as you got older.

You may begin to notice patterns in thoughts, behaviors or relationships that developed after the painful sexual experiences. For example, harmful ways in which your experience has impacted the way you interact in intimate relationships may become more clear. Or difficulties in sexual functioning may become more salient as you begin telling your story and examining the impact of the sexual abuse or unwanted experiences.

Although it can feel overwhelming to identify the impact of what happened to you, we have hope that our past does not define us. However, we cannot begin to heal if we do not assess the damage. Pretending everything is fine does not mean that everything *is* fine. Telling the truth allows us to present our broken selves to God and ask him to be with us in that brokenness, as well as to clearly show us the path to healing and restoration. By identifying the impact, we specifically look at how abuse has affected our identity, our sexual behavior, our bodies and our minds.

Rewrite your story. Ultimately, healing from sexual abuse is about rewriting your story. This happened to you, and it was wrong and awful. But you do not have to live in it now. You can learn new ways of relating, thinking, feeling and behaving. You can learn when and how to trust. You can learn to give and receive touch. You can learn to identify triggers, practice relaxation and speak truth to yourself.

For example, if you begin to have an angry response to your husband when he initiates sexual intimacy, you can remind yourself: "I am an adult and can choose how to respond—and this is my husband who I love. He is not trying to demean or hurt me. This is not disgusting but a beautiful expression of God's love." I am not suggesting a quick fix, as saying these words to yourself once will not magically cure your sexual relationship. But it is a first step.

Rewriting your story means telling the truth to yourself—that who you are is not what happened to you. Rather, who you are is who you are becoming in Christ. Telling yourself these truths over and over again will help you continue to rewrite your story in the present day instead of allowing the past to control your pen. Your sexual abuse and unwanted sexual experiences cannot be erased, and pretending they did not happen does not facilitate healing. They do *not*, however, have to define your future. The God who created us as sexual beings also "heals the brokenhearted / and binds up their wounds" (Psalm 147:3). We have a God who sees our pain and grieves with us, healing us with his own wounds and walking with us into the light.

8

Sexual Disappointment

Married or single, we all long for connection—
to fully love and be loved, to know and be fully known.
Marriage does not guarantee that kind of fulfillment;
neither does being single and able to pursue
meaningful friendships with any and all.
We are presumptuous to assume that either
singleness or marriage will fulfill us, yet we despair
if we assume we will not find some fulfillment
either in our marriage or our singleness.

Lisa Graham McMinn,
Sexuality and Holy Longing

When I was pregnant with my first child I used to imagine what
it would be like once our baby boy arrived. Images from Gerber
commercials invaded my mind as I pictured my husband and I snug-
gling each other and our little one, holding hands and gazing into
our baby's eyes. With eyes welling up with tears, we would admire
each other for the beautiful child we had created.

Thankfully, we did have moments like those—and they were precious and sacred—but we also had other kinds of moments. Moments like the night when, after having not slept more than three hours in a row for weeks, I was wandering the house at 4:00 a.m. with an infant emitting blood-curdling screams into my ear after having fed, rocked, changed, and done any number of dance moves and lullabies for him. Instead of sweet looks of appreciation at my husband for his fine baby-making skills, I gruffly woke him and almost tossed the baby at him while barking, "You take him now!" Although this is a scene that many parents may relate to, it is not the stuff of baby-food commercials.

MYTH: YOU MUST EXPERIENCE EROTIC SEXUAL SATISFACTION TO BE FULFILLED

Sometimes reality does not meet our expectations. So it is with our sexuality. Most of us grow up assuming that our life will lead to a Hollywood-style Happily Ever After: we will meet a great guy, get married, buy a nice house and have some cute kids. In the fairy tale, couples always still feel as sexually attracted to each other as the day they met. They have an exciting and spontaneous sex life, in which each partner has as much great sex as they want.

What happens when the realities of life do not meet our expectations? Although sexuality is a gift, and it is good—that may not necessarily be what sexuality *feels* like to us. Perhaps you have never married and are tired of feeling like you have no outlet for your sexual desires and longings for intimacy. Maybe you are single again after being divorced or widowed, and you are missing the opportunity for sexual expression inherent in marriage. Perhaps you are currently married but disappointed in your sexual relationship because of boredom, pain, dysfunction or lack of desire. Perhaps your frustration is related to your partner's desire or sexual performance. Or maybe you are experiencing the challenge of living as a sexual being in the midst of challenges like infertility, pregnancy or menopause.

While we may long to experience our sexuality as God designed it, the reality of our lives and circumstances sometimes leads to feelings of isolation, disappointment and guilt. We think we're getting the Gerber baby, and instead we get the up-all-night-screamer. What are some of the sources of disappointment and confusion in our lived experiences of sexuality? How can we grow in wholeness in our sexuality in the midst of such disappointment?

SEXUALITY AND THE SINGLE WOMAN

Ann is a single forty-year-old woman who has never married, and her sexuality does not always feel like a gift. She longs for the intimacy and companionship of a partner, and she sometimes feels incomplete as a single person. She is a strong, smart woman with a good career and fulfilling hobbies. She has good friends, but most of them are married with children, and she sometimes feels like an outsider. Her unmet sexual desires sometimes feel like a painful taunting, but she feels guilty and disappointed when she engages in sexual behaviors outside of marriage.

Although single folks may feel alone, the truth is that singlehood is becoming a much more common way of life for adults in American culture. Over 40 percent of Americans over the age of eighteen are single—meaning they either have never married or they are divorced or widowed.[1] In 1950, 78 percent of households were made up of married couples; today less than half (48 percent) of all households are composed of married couples.[2] Despite the growing number of adult singles, we still live in a Jerry Maguire world, where the "You-complete-me" fantasy prevails. Our world is oriented toward couples, and if you are "unlucky" enough to be alone, our culture seems to say, then any number of products are available to help you attract the man of your dreams: try this weight loss program, use that face cream or sign up for this dating website, and you, too, can have a Happily Ever After.

Many of the single women I've seen in counseling struggle with a belief that they are incomplete on their own. When a single woman overhears a friend's husband refer to his wife as his better half, what does that mean for her? Is a single woman only half a person? M. Gay Hubbard wrote, "One old and powerful myth is that a woman is incomplete in herself because she is female and that she needs a male to make her life and herself complete. The myth teaches women that regardless of the quality of her friendships or the depth and strength of relationships she may have, she is incomplete without a male."[3]

Returning to Ann—my single client who is a successful woman with good friends and close family relationships—she recently received a promotion at work, completed a marathon after months of training and returned from a life-giving vacation with a dear friend. However, despite all these wonderful aspects of her life, which she sees and recognizes, she recently broke down in tears in my office because of her overwhelming feelings of failure and loneliness. The tears were unusual since Ann is typically somewhat stoic, but on this day, her sadness was palpable. Ann cannot escape the feeling that something is fundamentally wrong with her since she has not found a partner. Although Ann's life is filled with good things, she struggles at times with defining her identity solely on something she does not have—a husband.

On a daily basis, women are affirmed and valued for externals— our successful career, our beauty and appearance, our husband and children. As women, we are called to reflect God's loving, relational nature to the world around us in our work and relationships. For a married woman, this includes the role of a wife, but a woman's primary identity is still as a child of God and sister in Christ. For single women, whether never married or previously married, your primary identity, too, is always as a child of God and sister in Christ.

Acknowledging our primary identity as children of God does not automatically erase feelings of sadness or disappointment for single women—no more than it erases feelings of disappointment regarding marriage for the married woman. Feelings of isolation or inadequacy should be spoken and grieved. For women who are divorced or widowed, making the transition in identity from single to married back to single can be difficult in unique ways. The challenge for all of us—whether single or married—is in continually reminding ourselves of our primary identity as children of God, and asking God how to best live out our callings in this place, in this moment, in this season of our lives.

SINGLENESS AND COMMUNITY

Whether married or single, our God-given sexuality creates the drive in us to know and be known by another, to give ourselves in loving relationships, and to find real and intimate connection with others. For individuals who are married, the primary outlet for this drive toward intimacy is typically with one's spouse. For single individuals, those longings are often directed toward others in friendship.

One of the challenges facing singles searching for real community is found in our nuclear-family-centric churches. Whether women have never been married or are divorced or widowed, community can be a challenge. As a single woman without kids, Ann participates in the small singles group at her church, but she often wishes for more opportunity to connect with mixed groups. Her church, however, is mostly comprised of families, and she often feels like the third (or fourth or fifth) wheel at church functions. Although the church is meant to be a place of worship for the family of God, it sometimes feels more like a place of worship for nuclear families. Programming is directed toward a particular kind of family demographic, which leaves many single adults feeling like they will only become a fully participating member of the church if they have a spouse and a child.

Because the church is made up of folks who are, first, brother and sister in Christ, those of us who are married can and should look for opportunities to foster relationships with all others, including singles, in the family of God. As a married mom with a house full of energetic (read: loud) kids, I am sometimes guilty of assuming that my single friends would not want to be included in my domestic life. Women and men who are married, like me, need to give our single friends a chance to be included in our lives and communities—and allow the friends to make the choice whether to put up with our noise and chaos. We also need to allow our single friends to invite us into their lives. The community that arises out of different life experiences and journeys is a richer reflection of God's unity and diversity.

My friend Kate is twenty-seven and single, and she put it this way in a recent email conversation: "I want others (especially those in the church) to view me as whole and valuable even if I'm single, maybe even because I'm single. I want the preacher to stop addressing the single people in the congregation by saying, 'When you get married, you'll understand.' What if I understand despite being unmarried? And is there a money-back guarantee for that 'when'? Don't feel sorry for me—just share your life with me." Kate's challenge reminds us of our human need for covenant relationships and the call to live that out—whether we happen to be married or single.

SINGLENESS AND SEXUAL BEHAVIOR

Our sexuality drives us toward intimacy, but it also drives us toward . . . sex. Christian single women are often left wondering what to do with physical longings for sexual expression. To complicate matters further, Christian singles live in a world with diametrically opposed messages regarding sexual behavior. On one side of this dichotomy is our hypersexual culture, which assumes that all normal adults will engage in sexual behavior, especially when characters in the movies are given sympathy from their single friends if they have gone a month without sex. Here the notion of abstaining from sex is viewed as unthinkable and unhealthy.

On the other side of this dichotomy is the traditional teaching of the church—that sex is reserved for marriage. While in many churches, no other outlets or suggestions are offered for sexual urges or longings, the "Just say no!" message remains clear. For singles who are in committed romantic relationships, figuring out appropriate physical boundaries can be confusing and frustrating. For singles without a dating partner, knowing what to do with those physical urges can be even more complicated. Women who were previously married may find it difficult to suddenly shut down their sexual urges after being free to act on them within marriage.

When I talk with single women about their frustrations, we often talk about ways to be *for* something positive with their bodies, instead of just trying to work *against* their sexual urges. When people want to lose weight, it can help to focus on what they need more of—nutrient-rich foods, lean proteins, exercise and so on—rather than just obsessing about what they can't have or merely counting calories and restricting food. Likewise, when we focus on the positive things we are moving toward in our lives, it can shift our perspective and help us see the good we are pursuing—rather than just feeling frustrated by the physical urges we are choosing not to act on for immediate gratification at this moment.

For some women, reframing their struggle and changing the language they use to describe their behavior can be helpful. For example, when folks say, "I'm waiting for marriage to have sex," this implies a failure to reach a goal and also reinforces a false expectation that marriage is the reward for purity. Instead, singles may choose to focus on pursuing a spiritual discipline like chastity. *Chastity* is an old-fashioned word that has been revived recently, and with good reason:

> It is purity in conduct and intention. It is not the absence of sexuality, or sexual feelings. These remain intact. . . . Chastity is not the suppression of sexuality. Your body and your hormones will want to do their thing and there is little you can do to stop them. The whole concept of chastity only makes sense

in the presence of a raging sex drive. If you have no drive what-soever, *chastity* is not the right term. . . . Chastity, then, is a set of choices that one determines to make.[4]

All women, married or single, make choices about sexual behavior in light of who they are as children of God and sisters in Christ. But as a single woman, if you choose to refrain from bodily sexual intimacy with another person, then you are choosing *for* something (chastity), not just *against* having sex.

Single women can also actively seek out ways to live in and enjoy their bodies. Ann and I spent a lot of time talking about how her running and training served as an outlet for some sexual urges, though it was also a way she was able to grow increasingly comfortable in her own skin. I encourage the women I see in counseling to look for ways to participate in the world around them with their minds, hearts and bodies, which can mean anything from tae kwon do to knitting, from belly dancing to gourmet cooking. Instead of seeing the body as something whose drives and impulses must be battled against and defeated, all of these are ways to live in and *enjoy* one's body.

Many women also use more distinctly sensual activities, such as masturbation, as a way to cope with sexual feelings. As discussed earlier, Christians often grow up with a black-and-white understanding of masturbation in which it is viewed as "all bad"—an oversimplified response. In the area of sexual behavior, in particular, masturbation can sometimes be helpful in coping with sexual feelings.

We are embodied creatures, and when we acknowledge that and live in it, we recognize and appreciate the gift God has given us. At the same time, it is essential to acknowledge the disappointment and pain of loss, and not being able to express one's physical and sexual urges is a loss. Learning how to live with, grieve, and learn from loss is an essential part of any journey toward healing and wholeness.

SEXUALITY AND THE MARRIED WOMAN

Theologians have long discussed the creational purposes of sexual union within marriage. Several of these were discussed in chapter 2 and are worth briefly reviewing here. Sex is *uniting*, joining husband and wife into a one-flesh relationship. Sex is *fruitful*, providing couples with the opportunity to welcome children into the world. Sex is *pleasurable*, and the pleasure of sex is not incidental but God-created. For many married folks, however, sex does not *feel* uniting, fruitful or pleasurable. Although marriage provides the Christian boundary within which sexual union is deemed appropriate, many married women struggle with disappointment in their sexuality.

Roberta has been married for seventeen years, and although she remembers enjoying sex early in their marriage, it has long since become an afterthought. Between working and caring for their two children, she is often exhausted. She knows her husband wishes they would have sex more frequently, and she feels guilty that she doesn't initiate sex more with her husband. Although sex is meant to bring Roberta and her husband into a one-flesh relationship, more often than not she feels disconnected because of the busyness of their life.

There are many reasons why married women may not experience the uniting purpose of sexual union. For example, couples may be disconnected because of lack of communication, lack of emotional intimacy, or because of built-up resentment and hurt. When couples have experienced infidelity or broken trust in some way, sex can feel like a reminder of their disconnection, rather than a uniting act of love. When either the wife or the husband desires sex much more frequently than the other, frustration and disappointment can build up on both sides. Instead of feeling like a unifying act, sex can become a battlefield, where it feels as if one partner "winning" means the other one is "losing."

As we know, sex is intended to be a life-uniting act, reminding us of the commitment we have made to live in a covenantal, monogamous relationship with one particular person. Like baptism, it is a sign of both a love we are receiving and a commitment we are making to another. Sex, however, does not do the work of intimacy. As Margaret and Dwight Peterson point out:

> As counterintuitive as it may seem (at least to those caught up in the restless quest for more and better), sexual satisfaction is not about novelty. It is about connection, relationship and openness to intimacy. True eroticism is not incompatible with familiarity. True eroticism is grounded in the kind of mutual surrender that can be enacted only by partners who have learned or are in the process of learning to trust each other with their lives and with their bodies.[5]

Sex reminds us of who we are and how we are to live, but it is not intimacy or life itself. In other words, when couples do not experience sex as uniting, it may be helpful to look for disconnected areas within one's whole life and marriage. Much like physical pain provides a signal that trouble lurks somewhere within the body, disconnected sex can provide a signal that trouble lurks somewhere in the marriage. Rather than expecting sex to fix the problem, couples can look for ways to connect in other areas of their marriage first. Marriage counseling can be an incredibly helpful way for couples to identify patterns of disconnection, as well as learning new ways of creating and maintaining intimacy and connection. As one's marriage becomes more united and connected, the sexual relationship is likely to *feel* more uniting.

WHEN YOU CANNOT CONCEIVE

Laura is a thirty-three-year-old woman who has been trying to conceive a child with her husband for four years. She believes sexuality is a gift, and she wholeheartedly wants to experience the procreational purpose of sex—to welcome a child into their family. Regardless of their efforts and desire, however, no pregnancy ensues. Sex has become a scheduled, medicalized act, prescribed by doctors at particular times. Her husband feels a constant pressure to perform, and each sex act feels like a reminder of their failure and disappointment. Not only does Laura's sexual relationship feel like a failure, but sometimes that sense of failure bleeds over into Laura's identity as a woman. She listens to women she loves and respects talk about how God has "called" them to be mothers, and she wonders why that calling does not seem to be for her as well. Every year on Mother's Day, Laura sits in painful silence as the moms in the church are asked to stand and be honored, and she wonders if she is less valuable as a woman who is *not* a mother. Laura's friends and family members know about her fertility struggle and offer support and encouragement, but Laura becomes weary of feeling pitied and having her personal disappointments be so public. And the years of negative pregnancy tests have taken a toll on her marriage; she longs to feel connected to her husband again—physically, spiritually and emotionally.

Folks experience bodily brokenness in all sorts of ways, and infertility is one of them. For Laura and her husband, they have had to grieve the possibility that their sexual relationship may never lead to children. They have also spent a lot of time praying over ways to experience marital fruitfulness in other ways. Laura and her husband recently began the adoption process and hope to welcome a child into their home that way. They also look for ways to live out fruitfulness and hospitality in their church and community. Despite the pain and disappointment of infertility, Laura and her husband are intentionally trying to live and appreciate the life they have, instead of living in what they do *not* have. This is much easier said than done, and some days are still filled with tears and anger.

Laura and her husband are also trying to remember that fruitfulness is not the *only* purpose of sex. After years of focusing on that aspect alone, they are working to rediscover the uniting and pleasurable aspects of sex. This is a process, and one practical intervention that can help a couple re-experience physical intimacy actually sounds somewhat counterintuitive. I encourage couples to engage in a set time with a "no intercourse" rule. During that period, couples can spend as much time as they want kissing, touching or being sexual—as long as there is no possibility of getting pregnant. This kind of sexual play can be incredibly intimate, but by removing the possibility of pregnancy, it can also lessen the feelings of disappointment and failure associated with sex.

WHEN MARRIED SEX IS NOT PLEASURABLE

Janie is a twenty-five-year-old woman who has been married for two years. She and her husband waited to have sex until they got married, but despite their best efforts she has never been able to reach orgasm in their lovemaking. She enjoys being intimate with her husband, but she feels like something is wrong with her. Even though she did the "right thing" and waited for sex, she has not gotten the rewarding sex life she expected.

God created women's bodies anatomically to experience sexual pleasure. Some of us, according to Clifford and Joyce Penner, grew up learning that "a woman is to be the passive recipient of the man's sexual desire. Women were created with vaginas as a receptacle for the sperm and seminal fluid of the man, you may reason; should this not make the woman a passive receiver of the man's aggression, rather than an active participant?" However, they argue, "The presence of the clitoris counters this attitude. The clitoris is the only organ in the human anatomy designed solely for receiving and transmitting sexual stimuli. Physiologically that is the *only* function. The woman, not the man, was created with the clitoris. . . . God intended women to be intensely sexual beings, not just 'vaginas' to receive the man's sexual expression."[6]

However, despite how God has created women and our bodies, this does not mean that all women feel pleasure in their sexual relationship. Some of us grew up with the idea that the reward for sexual purity while we were single was great sex once we were married. This myth intensifies feelings of frustration for married women who find that they do not physically enjoy sex the way they thought they would after watching Hollywood love scenes.

Inability to experience orgasm, however, is not the only source of sexual dissatisfaction in marriage. Grace is a fifty-two-year-old woman who is in her second marriage. Her current husband is a kind and gentle man who treats her with a tenderness and respect she never knew in her first marriage. Their sexual relationship, however, often feels bland and boring. He is uncomfortable with anything other than the missionary position, and he often has difficulty maintaining an erection. Grace feels guilty for sometimes missing the pleasure in her sexual relationship with her first husband, but she longs for a more sexually satisfying relationship with her current husband.

Couples may be struggling because one or both partners lack desire for sex, or they may even feel disgusted or repulsed by sex. Women may have difficulty experiencing sexual arousal or may experience pain during intercourse. Men may experience premature ejaculation or erectile dysfunction. Despite the variety of sexual functioning problems that couples may face, the good news is that they are treatable. Couples who are committed to improving their sexual relationship can read a book together on sexual functioning[7] or get help from a marriage counselor or sex therapist. With education and practice, couples experiencing these problems can see dramatic improvement.

Regardless of the avenue couples choose for improving their sexual relationship, a few areas to explore together might include the following.

Sensuality. Begin by learning to experience the world in a more sensory way. Pay attention to smells and tastes. Notice what things are pleasing to you and to your body. This is especially helpful for difficulties with sexual desire or arousal. Attend to the kinds of fabrics that feel good against your skin and the kinds of touch that feel safe and pleasurable, such as holding hands or a gentle hug. Be intentional about thinking sexual thoughts, and dismiss unhelpful self-talk, such as, "Oh, this is awful — he's going to want to have sex now." Instead, remind yourself that God has created you and your husband as sexual beings, and that it is a beautiful gift (which is what sex is, even if it doesn't feel that way right now).

Your body. For many women, problems stem from a lack of knowledge about our own anatomy and physiology. Many women grow up in a culture of shame about our external genitals. I remember when my four-year-old son came home from a playdate and told me, "Katie doesn't have a penis; she has a hoo-hoo. What's that, Mom?" Although this may sound like a silly story about preschoolers, I worry about the real-life impact of little girls not knowing the anatomically correct names for their genitals. What does it mean psychologically if we are uncomfortable even saying aloud the names of our body parts? Every year when I teach on sexuality, I see college females who are unable to sit through a class without squirming when I use the word *vagina*. If I ask female students what they call their genitals, the most common response is "down there." This level of discomfort with our own bodies — and even the *words* for our bodies — can certainly affect our sexual functioning.

A common sex therapy assignment for a woman is to use a mirror to examine your external genitalia. Clearly identify where your inner and outer labia are, as well as your clitoris. Use your hand to explore different levels of pressure to help you identify the pleasure/pain threshold. As you understand your own body more, you will be better able to guide your partner. So not only can you improve your sexual relationship by learning about your female body in general, but you can also learn more about how men's and women's bodies come to-gether in sexually intimate moments. Too often, we assume that when we are married, great sex should just happen naturally, without effort or conversation. If we have to talk about it or read a book, then something is wrong. This is an oversimplification and leads couples to withdraw from each other and from sex. Instead, learning about sex with your spouse can open doors to greater levels of physical and emotional intimacy.

Intimacy. Ultimately, sexual dysfunctions are always, on some level, about intimacy. Learning to have open and honest conversations with your spouse about what is sexually satisfying or not may seem awkward or embarrassing at first, but the potential benefits are great. Difficulties in sexual functioning are often about trust and safety. By building trust, you will increase the potential for satisfying sex in marriage. It is unreasonable to expect to connect physically when you are not connecting emotionally.

One of the things my husband and I suggest to the couples we counsel—more than anything else—is to have weekly date nights. Couples often have a list of reasons why that is impossible, but we believe prioritizing your marriage is one of the best things you can do for your family. Dates don't have to include five-star restaurants. A date night can mean spreading a blanket on the floor and having a frozen-pizza picnic after the kids are in bed. We have seen the pos-itive impact of creating intentional time together in our clients' mar-riages, as well as in our own. I love my husband's commitment to this weekly date night. Although it takes planning and financial sacrifice, it also keeps our marriage alive. It is often not until we are sitting across the table from each other over coffee or dinner on our date night that we realize we haven't had a real conversation all week. Getting away from the tasks of the house and the demands of our children, we are able to ask each other questions and truly listen to each other. Emotional intimacy paves the way for physical intimacy, and it allows sex to be a more accurate representation of the one-flesh reality of marriage.

LEARNING TO LOVE

While it was easy to love my baby when he looked, sounded and smelled like the commercials on TV, it was harder when he was screaming at 3 a.m. But this is real love, isn't it? Love loves when it's tough. When we experience the beauty of our sexuality in the butterflies of first love or in the passionate throes of honeymoon nights, it is easy to celebrate our sexuality. When life confronts us with difficulties and disappointment, the real work begins.

God is interested in growing us up in Christ, and our sexuality is one of those transformational tools, shaping us into individuals who can truly love. Lewis Smedes puts it this way: "Sexuality is a drive that begins in our glands and climaxes in communion. . . . Personal communion is what the image of God is about. Biblical revelation tells us to stop thinking of ourselves as isolated islands of rational Godlikeness and think of ourselves instead as coming into real humanity when we live in genuine personal fellowship with others."[8] In other words, our sexuality is not ultimately about having sex or having good sex. Sexuality is about connection and communion with others. Perhaps the disappointments we experience in our sexuality can also serve us as we learn to truly create community with others and await ultimate union with Christ.

9

Redemptive Sexuality

If everything that I've gone through
in my life had to happen in order
for us to save this baby here . . .
it was all worth it.

Lisa Williams,
CNN online

Lisa Williams is a strong and successful businesswoman, wife and mother, but she is also a survivor of the kind of trauma that most of us only read about in the newspaper. As a young child, Lisa was sexually abused by an older relative. When Lisa was eleven, a friend of her mother's told Lisa he could sell her for a few dollars. When that same man later tried to rape Lisa and physically assaulted her so profoundly that she was hospitalized, Lisa's mother declined to press charges. Instead she dropped the then-twelve-year-old Lisa off at the bus station, and Lisa spent her adolescent years on the streets: "When I didn't have a job I sold myself so that I could eat. After all, that's what I had been groomed to do. . . . That was my value. That was my worth."[1]

Despite all the ways in which Lisa's body and sexuality were abused, demeaned and degraded, she is a beautiful example of redemptive sexuality. Lisa eventually found her way off the streets: she graduated from college, earned a master's degree, became an engineer and a successful businesswoman. With all her successes, however, Lisa never forgot or allowed herself to become numb to the suffering of others. Several years ago, Lisa saw a news story about a ten-year-old girl who was being charged with prostitution—with no mention of the men who bought or sold her—and she was enraged: "It's as if [the law] was saying she woke up that morning and decided she wanted to be sold to 10 to 15 men. . . . That just didn't make sense to me."[2] Lisa noticed the subtext in this article of victim-blaming, and she was unable to ignore it.

Many of us have become emotionally affected after watching particular news stories or reading articles, but let's be honest about what we often do: we think about it for a few days, and then we go on with our daily lives. Not Lisa Williams. Lisa allowed herself to be moved to action. The article Lisa read mentioned a safe house for prostituted girls, so Lisa called friends all over the country to raise money for the safe house. Then Lisa learned there were not enough safe houses to meet the need: "It was my God nudging me, saying 'What part of six beds east of the Mississippi did you not hear?'"[3] So Lisa started a nonprofit organization called Circle of Friends, and in 2008, they bought a three-story house in Georgia. Less than two years later, Lisa's safe house (Living Water for Girls) for up to ten formerly prostituted girls opened its doors.

MYTH: SEXUALITY IS ABOUT THE INDIVIDUAL

In Lisa Williams's story, we see a powerful example of God's redemptive work. God can and does redeem us *from* shame and sin, but that is not the end of the story. He redeems us *to* love—to reflect the shape of God's love in our lives, our relationships and our communities. As God has redeemed Lisa from the shame of her past, he has also redeemed her to love deeply and to live out that love in real and tangible ways. Lisa's story reminds us that our discussions about sexuality and womanhood should not ultimately *just* be about us—about our personal growth or healing or knowledge—but also about how we are being changed for others.

Our individual sexual healing is one part of the whole drama of God restoring humanity and creation to himself. The point of reflecting on these issues—how we learn about sex, wounds we have incurred, and how we can grow and heal from those wounds—is to be able to participate more fully in God's story of redemption. Our sexuality, by definition, is what God uses to transform us from self-centered to self-giving, opening the circle of our own love and intimacy.

God grows us up not only for ourselves but *for others*. Throughout this book, we have explored pathways to healing and wholeness in our sexuality. The beautiful message of redemption is that God can and does use our wounds to be a source of healing for others. This does *not* mean God caused those hard things, but we *can* trust that God makes light out of darkness. And that light is not meant only for you or me but for a hurting world. Sometimes the most redemptive work we can do is to receive God's love and restoration. Allowing ourselves time to grieve and begin the healing process is not selfish. On the contrary, that resting time better equips us to reach out to others in more selfless and authentic ways when the time comes.

In the big picture, we should not just be interested in our own or our partner's sexual healing, but in the brokenness and restoration of *all* those in need of healing. In this chapter we will examine what it means to truly live out God's call to self-giving, self-sacrificial love. God redeems us from shame and sin so that we can love more deeply. To really see that, we will explore the shape of God's love and how God uses our sexuality to grow us up in Christ in order to live out that love in relationship with others.

REDEEMED FROM SHAME

Lisa Williams's childhood was filled with shame and pain, but her story does not end there. Instead, God's redemptive work allowed Lisa to move past her own story and enter into the pain and shame of other people's stories. Lisa could have lived the rest of her life in a place of anger—toward her mother for abandoning her, or toward the men who misused and abused her—and no one would have blamed her. She had every reason to be angry, and who could possibly suggest that she just get over it and move on? Yet if Lisa had remained lost in her story, her abusers would have won. How much healing would she have missed out on—not to mention what would have become of the girls of Living Water or the community that was inspired by her actions? Lisa knew and grieved her story and her pain, but she did not stay there.

The wound of sexual shame touches us deeply because it affects our core personhood. When we face deep hurt in our lives, the temptation is to get bogged down by it. Despite our longing to move on, we may feel lost in anger, bitterness, resentment or hurt. When we face deep hurt, we cannot and should not simply say we are fine and keep going. Like a physical wound, deep healing of sexual wounds requires us to confront the hurt and examine the damage. Only then can we apply the appropriate ointments—rather than ignoring the wound, allowing it to fester and grow into something even worse. Healing requires us to look inside and to know ourselves—our pain, our hurts and our stories—but we can and should move outside ourselves.

The deep hurt of sexual shame can make us feel broken, but God calls us to allow our wounds to transform us and grow us into something more than we were before. When we allow God to do his work in us, we allow that pain to move us outside ourselves so that we can more clearly see the hurt in our brothers' and sisters' eyes.

Rather than remaining in our own stories of pain or betrayal, we can begin to see the suffering around us. Reaching outside ourselves is actually good medicine for our own wounds too, because being part of helping someone else helps us too. God has created us for community, and when we participate in that community of healing, the benefits fall on us all. God redeems us from shame in his deep love for us, and in that redemptive work, allows us to reach out in love toward others.

REDEEMED FROM SIN

God redeems us from the wounds that others have inflicted on us, but he also redeems us from our own sin. Some of the shame we experience is due to our own choices. Jenny is a forty-four-year-old married woman with two children. She and her husband have struggled for years with physical and emotional intimacy, and she often blamed their problems on her sexual promiscuity as a teenager. In the early years of their marriage, both she and her husband also had extramarital affairs. As they are working to rebuild their marriage, her guilt and shame regarding her sexual sin often leads to feelings of hopelessness regarding their future. However, God frees us from sin and shame in order to grow us up in Christ.

Our sexuality, in and of itself, is far from sinful. God created it, and it is a good reflection of his love and character. When we abuse, worship or demean it, however, that is sinful, and it drives a wedge between us and God, separating us. Because our sexuality is so connected to our core personhood, the scars that sexual sin leaves behind can run deep.

Sexual sin goes against the will of God, which is for sex to be contained in the covenant faithfulness of marriage. Sexual sin also goes against the work of God, which is done when sex is a uniting, self-giving sign that points to our ultimate union with Christ. Sin creeps in when sex takes place outside of marriage, or it can manifest itself when sexuality is selfish or demeaned and depersonalized, when it is about getting something for oneself—whether pleasure, release, approval or a relationship. God created sex to be a reflection of his love, which is life-giving and sacrificial.

Shame, guilt and pain from sexual sin, past or present, can feel overwhelming. We may connect with David's words, "For I know my transgressions, / and my sin is always before me" (Psalm 51:3). Yet we can also stand with David when he speaks truth about God's character: "Cleanse me with hyssop, and I will be clean; / wash me, and I will be whiter than snow" (Psalm 51:7). God is growing us up in him. He forgives our sin and shows us a better way to live in him. Thankfully, we have the freedom to align our behavior with who God is and who we truly are in Christ. Like a good parent, God does not leave us where we are at, but he tenderly leads us to a better place.

Dealing with sin in our lives is the essence of the sanctification process, by which God shapes us into Christlike children. Turning away from sin begins with confession, which is not the kind of exhibitionistic disclosure that takes place on daytime talk shows or Facebook proclamations. Rather, confession refers to a deep acknowledgment of the sin in one's heart and life.

When we confess our sin to ourselves, to God and to another person, we bring that darkness into the light. We invite God to love us more, to shape us into who he wants us to become in him. Because God created us in his image to be relational beings, when we confess our sin to another, we open the door for accountability and community, where true change can happen in relationship. When we confess and open ourselves to God and to others, we allow and invite them to journey with us—where we can turn away from the sin and do something different.

REDEEMED TO LOVE

In one of the most familiar passages in the Bible, the shape of God's love is described perfectly: "For God so loved the world that he gave his one and only Son, that whoever believes in him shall not perish but have eternal life" (John 3:16). God *so* loved that he *gave*; this is the essence of God's sacrificial love.[4] God has a nature, and that nature is love. God's love is defined by covenant faithfulness. It is not turned in on itself but opens itself up: "God so loved the world." Because it is fruitful and life-giving, those who receive his love are given life forever with him.

As we seek to reflect the shape of God's love in our own lives, we can ask ourselves: What do we *so love?* My eight-year-old son so loves video games that his perfect day would be a marathon of the Wii, iPad and computer. When we first explained why excessive video-game time is not good for him, he responded with, "But this is just the way I am!" Similarly, we all have things that get in the way of God growing us up in Christ—even if this example just seems like a little kid trying to get his way. So I ask, What do you *so love* that you spend excessive time or energy pursuing it? Perhaps you love shopping, being liked, being on Facebook, being right, getting attention from men, working out, drinking wine, Pinterest or sex? If I look at my life, my heart, my struggle and my sin, and if I say to God, "This is just the way I am," then I am asking God to stop his work in me. I am essentially asking him to love me less, not more!

God is love, and love loves to perfection. Love that leaves us where we are is not really love. So while God meets us where we are at, he also gently and inexorably takes us to where we are going. One can envision God as the artist who is continually redrawing us. When we justify ourselves as just being how we are, then we keep God from transforming us into who we can be in Christ.

We know sexuality is about who we *are* as women created in God's image, but it is also about who we are becoming and how we *live*— whether we are young or old, married or single. When we consider principles for holy sexual living in our world, we need to build on the foundation of the shape of God's love, rather than on the distorted messages of our popular culture or our own personal histories. Our sexuality offers lessons about our lives now, as well as a picture of the lives we were ultimately created for, where we have union with Christ. As we seek to reflect God's love in our daily lives, several foundational principles can be guideposts for us.

Celebrate your sexuality. When our sexuality has been a source of guilt, shame or pain, we may feel like our sexuality itself is painful, shameful or guilt-inducing. But even though it might feel painful or disappointing, the truth is that our sexuality is actually a good thing.

Our identity as sexual beings is foundational to how God has uniquely created us in his image. Becoming healthy, whole women means learning to listen to our uniquely female sexuality without denying, misusing, manipulating, worshiping or rejecting it. We are called to celebrate the gift of our sexuality—regardless of how free (or not) we are to express that gift in our sexual behavior if we are single or regardless of how satisfying our sexual relationship is if we are married. We can enjoy that God created us for intimacy, and re-member that our longing for it is a reminder of God's own longing for us. We can constantly be looking for ways to love sacrificially and to open the circle of our own love relationships.

Remember the goal. If this were a secular book on female sexu-ality, the goal would likely be to teach women how to have better sex and experience the erotic aspects of their sexuality in a more satis-fying way. And for those women who want to wait for marriage to have sex, the goal of that book might be to (a) convince the reader of the naivete of that belief, (b) help women find ways to experience erotic satisfaction alone or (c) help those women find a spouse so they can finally have sex. In Christian theology, all of those goals lead us away from the true purpose and beauty of our sexuality.

Although marriage and great sex are both worthwhile endeavors, they are not the whole picture. The goal of our sexuality is not mar-riage if you are single nor is it great sex if you are married. Rather, the deep and true purpose of sex is to serve as a reminder of what we were truly made for. When we remember that sex is a sign pointing to our eventual whole-self intimacy with Christ, we can be grounded. We can also be reminded that what our culture tells us is true and important is often misleading. By directing our eyes to Christ, we can ask God what our sexuality is teaching us about where he is leading us, to prepare us for eventual union with him.

Learn to receive love. The first thing we are called to do when we become believers in Christ is to receive and accept his love. Jesus continuously received from the Father, and this is what God wants us to do—receive his love. Unfortunately, pride often keeps us from truly receiving love from God and others. To freely receive from anyone is, in some ways, a small miracle. Being in the giving role can feel safer because it puts us in a position of power and control. When someone gives love to us, even in small ways, we are often driven to pay it back and make it even. If a friend buys us lunch, we mentally note that so we can buy the next time.

Receiving love means accepting that we are being given something we cannot give ourselves and cannot pay back. Submission is actually a willingness to receive, and in this way, we are all called to submit to God and to others. We cannot really give love to others unless we have first fully and truly received love. As 1 John 4:19 tells us, "We love because he first loved us."

Embrace the mystery. The messages we receive about our identity as gendered beings and what we do with that in our sexual behavior are varied. When we consider gender identity, gender roles, views on sexual practices for single and married folks, how to respond to questions about sexual orientation or masturbation, or about sexual freedom within marriage—it is easy to view sexuality as a complicated problem. Instead, we need to approach sexuality for what it is: a mystery.

When we embrace the mystery, we can move away from contradictory, black-and-white messages about sex in our churches and in popular culture, where sex is either evil or god. We can avoid viewing sexuality through the reductionistic lens where it is merely particular acts. Sexuality is a mystery to be approached with appreciation of God's creative power, not a problem to be solved with quick answers or political stances. Instead of searching for prescriptive formulas that can be applied to all, we can appreciate the fact that our sexuality is a dynamic, living representation of God's love being worked out in and through us.

BE FRUITFUL

"God *so* loved that he *gave* . . ." Our God-created sexuality is central to our identity as women who are made in God's image. One of the most important aspects of our sexuality is fruitfulness. Although one very obvious demonstration of this fruitfulness is when sexual union leads to children, fruitfulness goes far beyond procreation. As we explored earlier, fruitfulness means that God grows us, not just for our own sake but for the sake of others. With others, we can be a demonstration of the self-giving, sacrificial love that Jesus modeled. As individuals made in God's image, we have been created *for* others to be part of restoring God's whole community to himself. We may seek healing for ourselves, but God's path of healing always includes others along the way. Just as the Trinity does not simply stay within their circle of reciprocal love yet opens that circle to give life and love to us, so we are called to practice self-giving love in our own lives.

Jesus often taught his followers important truths through stories and parables. One of the most familiar of these is the parable of the Good Samaritan, where Jesus taught a powerful lesson about our first step to participating in God's redemptive story. Here, he set up a painful scene with a man who had been attacked, beaten, stripped and left on the side of the road. Jesus then described a priest who saw the man but "passed by on the other side" (Luke 10:31). Next, Jesus described a Levite who saw the wounded man, but he, too, "passed by on the other side" (v. 32). Finally, a Samaritan came upon the man "and when he saw him, he took pity on him" (v. 33). Jesus went on to describe how the Samaritan bandaged the man's wounds, took him to an inn and paid for his care. Of all the beautiful pieces of this story, perhaps the most stunning is how Jesus described the man. The hatred between Jews and Samaritans was so longstanding that the Samaritan's ethnicity made crossing the road to help the man even more shocking.

We are told that the priest and the Levite "see" the man, but then they quickly move to avoid him. Their actions reveal that the men never allowed themselves to truly *see* the hurting man at all. The priest and Levite were apparently so blinded by their agendas, plans and religious rules that they missed the greatest two rules of all: "'Love the Lord your God with all your heart and with all your soul and with all your mind and with all your strength.' The second is this: 'Love your neighbor as yourself'" (Mark 12:30-31).

This story may be so familiar to many of us that it is easy to skip over the priest and the Levite. We may be tempted to see them as the bad guys, without thinking too much about what they might have been thinking or feeling in the moment. Perhaps the priest was concerned that he would be late to some important priestly duty if he stopped to help the man. Although his motivation to do his priestly work may have been good, he missed the most important duty presented to him in that moment.

While the priest may have been contemplating his responsibilities, perhaps the Levite assumed that if the man had been beaten and bloodied, it was due to his own actions. This kind of thinking is what social psychologists call the just-world phenomenon, in which people assume that other people's suffering is really their own fault. For example, when an individual assumes that rape victims may have been "asking for it" by dressing or acting provocatively, this is the just-world phenomenon at work. As is also the case when people assume that all those who are on welfare or homeless are in that situation because of their own laziness or substance abuse. In other words, if something bad happens, you had it coming because of your own sin or actions.

We tend to blame others for their suffering, but we approach our own pain differently. When it comes to our own suffering, social psychologists observe that most of us succumb to the self-serving bias, where we blame our troubles on external sources—bad luck or the actions of others. The irony is that our fallen, human nature tends to blame other people for their own problems *and* to blame anyone but ourselves for our own problems. Jesus speaks directly to this by asking us to open our eyes and take responsibility for both others and ourselves. When we suffer and hurt, we can look to Jesus and ask him for help. When others suffer, we can and should see their suffering and respond.

While the priest and the Levite pass by the beaten man, what does the Good Samaritan do? Does he interview the man to discover the reasons for his suffering and find out if he is worthy of his time and help? No, he sees the man—his need and his suffering—and he responds to it immediately. When we love God, we love his people, who are our neighbors. If we love our neighbors, we do not ignore their suffering—we see it and we see them. We do not turn away in discomfort or guilt or frustration because of our other responsibilities, because before we can do anything to be part of moving others toward health and wholeness, we first have to open our eyes to see their suffering.

But I fear I am often like the priest and the Levite who were too busy, too distracted, too focused on their own journeys to slow down for the man in need. We must take off our blinders and be willing to experience the discomfort of seeing the world as it is—a place filled with immeasurable pain and hurt and injustice. In the face of suffering of this magnitude, we may feel helpless and want to hide from it. However, even though we cannot fix everything, we cannot do nothing. We cannot pretend it doesn't exist. We cannot be silent.

Fruitfulness means that we do something. We do not allow ourselves to become numb, but we allow God to move us to action. When we hear stories like Lisa Williams's about sexual abuse or human trafficking, it is tempting to compartmentalize them into a box labeled something like: *That's so sad, and I'm relieved that hasn't happened to me or my loved ones.* When we are confronted with stories about the damaging messages our media and advertising are handing us regarding women and sexuality, we may think, *This is wrong and hurtful, but I am just one person. I can't do anything.* None of us can end abuse, pornography, prostitution or the damaging images of women in the media on our own. And that is the point. God has created us for community, and it is in the company of others that we are able to work to bring God's kingdom to earth now.

As Christians, Jesus calls us to a life of loving action. Unfortunately, this is not the example the world sees of Christians today. In a national survey of young people, the three most common perceptions of Christians were antihomosexual (91 percent), judgmental (87 percent) and hypocritical (85 percent).[5] This research reflects a cultural reality that, as a group, Christians are often known for being *against* something or someone, rather than being *for* Jesus.

In 1 Corinthians 13, the famous love chapter of the Bible so often read at weddings, we are told, "If I speak in the tongues of men or of angels, but do not have love, I am only a resounding gong or a clanging symbol" (v. 1). So Paul goes on to describe love: patient, kind, keeps no record of wrongs, rejoices in truth, neither is envious, proud, self-seeking or easily angered, always protects, hopes, perseveres—love never fails (vv. 4-8). God is love and has given us this huge, expansive love as an amazing gift through his Son, but what do we do with it?

I worry that we sometimes receive that gift of love like my childhood dog, Mandy, used to receive the gift of a bone. She was grateful for the gift, loving and cherishing it. She did not ignore the gift or think it unimportant. Rather, she would take her gift, bury herself under the couch or in a corner, and would growl at anyone who came near. She was given a gift of love and valued it highly, but all we saw was hostility, anger and fear come out of her as a result of receiving the gift. Perhaps too many of us are acting like Mandy. We value the gift of God's extravagant love and salvation in our lives, but instead of responding with more love, we exude hostility, anger and fear in our attempt to protect the integrity of the gift.

I long for us to be people who receive God's love with open arms. My hope is that you will know you are loved by God, and that you will believe just as strongly that your neighbor is equally loved by God. I want you to know to the depths of your being that love is not just a gift you have been given, but it is a gift you are to be part of giving to the world. Bob Goff, in his book *Love Does*, suggests, "I think Jesus had in mind that we would not just be 'believers' but 'participants.' Not because it's hip, but because it's accurate, more fitting that way. He wanted people who got to the 'do' part of faith. . . . It's not about being politically correct; it's about being actually correct. We need to make our faith our very own love story."[6] If we have faith in a Savior who sacrificed himself for us, then that faith should manifest itself as a love story. When you love someone, you don't just think about them—you do something. If we are Christians, the world should know us by our love, and love does something.

Instead of focusing on all that we cannot do (solve the problem, change the system, etc.), we need to shift our attention to what we can do. We need to begin not with our own inadequacy or the enormity of the problem, but with prayer. Bring the suffering and pain you observe to the foot of Jesus and ask God, "What would you have me do?" Cornelius Plantinga Jr. writes, "To be a responsible person is to find one's own role and then, funded by the grace of God, to fill this role and to delight in it."[7] Your next step, funded by the grace of God, is waiting for you. So what is your next move? We cannot do everything, but we can do something.

God's love has the power to grow us up and transform us. God loves us now and is more tender with us than a mother with her newborn babe, but he also loves us too much to leave us alone in our sin and brokenness. I hope you will learn to receive God's love and be changed by it—"And I pray that you, being rooted and established in love, may have power, together with all the Lord's holy people, to grasp how wide and long and high and deep is the love of Christ, and to know this love that surpasses knowledge—that you may be filled to the measure of all the fullness of God" (Ephesians 3:17-19)—so that you can find your something, and go do it.

Appendix A

Going Deeper

A Guide for Growth and Reflection

Are you ready to have a different story about sexuality in your life? If you are eager to dig deeper into these ideas about sexuality and womanhood, and if you are ready to actively move toward new ways of seeing, thinking and behaving, then this guide is for you. It will provide in-depth questions and activities for each chapter, which should assist you on your journey toward whole sexuality.

Most of these activities will require a journal and some time alone for quiet reflection. For each activity, you should give yourself at least thirty minutes. Ideally, you will complete these activities independently, and then you will come together with a counselor, a friend or a safe group of women in order to process your experiences and insights together. For more about how to use these activities in a group, see appendix B.

CHAPTER 1: YOU ARE SEXUAL AND IT IS GOOD

Identify your sexuality lens. In this first exercise, I want to encourage you to intentionally reflect on how you were introduced to the behavioral and physiological components of sexuality. Without judging or evaluating your experiences, try to get a picture in your mind of the moment(s) you first learned about key sexual components. How did you first discover things like

- menstruation or your first period?

- boys having erections? wet dreams?

- masturbation?

- sexual activities, such as French kissing? foreplay? oral sex? sexual intercourse?

How old were you? Where were you? Who else was in the scene with you? Did you learn about it directly in a conversation, through a book, a picture or an observation of some sort? Did you overhear someone else, or did someone talk to you personally? If so, was it a parent, sibling or friend? Was it someone you knew and trusted, or was it someone who you didn't know or trust?

As you ask these questions and remember, attend to all five of your senses. What do you remember seeing? What did you hear? What did you feel, taste or smell? Describe what parts of the memories are most salient for you. Was it scary or safe? embarrassing or comfortable?

Our first exposure to sexuality often creates a lens through which later lessons about sexuality are filtered. So if our initial lessons about sexuality are shameful or embarrassing, we may find ourselves feeling a default emotional response of shame or embarrassment in later experiences of sexuality.

What words could describe your initial sexuality "lens"? In other words, how would you have completed these sentences?

- Having a period is _____.

- Sex is _____.

- When it comes to sexuality, girls and women are _____
_____.

- When it comes to sexuality, boys and men are _____
_____.

How do you think those early lessons about sexuality affected your feelings and thoughts about sex, men and women growing up? How do they affect your life today?

As an adult, you can choose to evaluate and modify the lens through which you view sexuality. No longer do you have to be subject to the model of sexuality you were introduced to in girlhood or adolescence. Take some time to reflect on those aspects of your implicit sexuality lens that you want to hold on to, as well as those it is time to discard. Then complete the following statement: *Regardless of my history—what I have thought, felt or done (or had done to me)—I want to experience sexuality as _____.*

CHAPTER 2: MORE THAN AN ACT

Create a personal sexuality model. You will need a large piece of paper to complete this exercise. Using the model of sexuality described in this chapter, think about ways you experience your sexual identity in your body, mind, social identity and behavior. If this exercise becomes too painful at any point, take a break and come back to it with the help and support of a trusted friend or counselor.

Using the Venn diagram on page 24 as a model, draw a center circle labeled "Core Self," along with four interlocking circles labeled "Body," "Mind," "Social Identity" and "Behavior." I recommend using the entire page for this exercise so you have space to write inside each of these circles.

Once you have each circle labeled, contemplate how you experience each of these components of your sexuality. Take your time with this exercise, and don't rush through it. These are questions and categories you probably do not typically use to conceptualize your identity and sexuality.

Set the diagram aside while you use your journal to respond to the questions below, reflecting on your journey toward sexual wholeness in each of these domains.

Body

- In my body, I feel broken because of _____ (*poor body image, eating problems, physical pain, exhaustion/fatigue, illness, etc.*).

- In my body I experience wholeness when I _____ (*care for it through exercise, allow myself to rest, enjoy food I love, go for walks, drink tea, take baths, etc.*).

Mind

- In my mind, I feel broken because of _____ (*feelings and thoughts about myself as a woman, my sexual and/or romantic fantasies, attraction to the wrong people, etc.*).

- In my mind I experience wholeness when I _____ (*embrace my identity as a woman, can identify and accept my longings for intimacy with another, focus my fantasies on my spouse, etc.*).

Social Identity

- In my social identity, I feel broken because of _____ (*how I experience my own "feminine" and "masculine" traits, how others respond to my masculinity/femininity, etc.*).

- In my social identity I experience wholeness when I _____ _____ (*interact with others in authentic ways, embrace my own strengths regardless of how "masculine" or "feminine" they are, etc.*).

Behavior

- In my behavior, I feel broken because of _____ (*past or current sexual choices, past or current unwanted sexual experiences from a stranger, friend or intimate partner, past or current sexual abuse, etc.*).

- In my behavior I experience wholeness when I _____
  *(behave in ways congruent with my beliefs and values, release myself
  from guilt for the choices of others, forgive myself for past behavior,
  etc.).*

After you have completed the questions above, choose two keywords or phrases for each domain to reflect your experiences of both
brokenness and wholeness. For example, under "Behavior," you
might choose the word *hookups* to reflect a way you have experienced
brokenness, as well as *forgiveness* to represent wholeness. Then write
those keywords in each circle, so in the "Behavior" circle, you would
write the words *hookups* and *forgiveness.*

Once you have completed the keywords for each of the four
circles, spend some time quietly reflecting on the whole page. Say
the keywords aloud, and ask yourself what message these words have
for you about your core selfhood. Choose a word or two that can
speak to the wholeness offered to you in Christ, and write it in the
center circle labeled "Core Self." Some possible words you might
choose could be: *loved, redeemed, clean, healthy, connected* and so
on. When you feel confused, frustrated or guilt-ridden, return to this
page to remind yourself of who you are in Christ and the ways in
which he is redeeming your story.

CHAPTER 3: BEYOND THE BATTLE OF THE SEXES

Assess your gender bias. In this chapter the male-centered versus
female-centered models of womanhood were discussed. This exercise
will help you flesh out your own working model of gender and sexuality. Respond to the following sentence prompts in your journal:

- I believe sex should happen _____ *(when?
  with whom?).*

- In my own life, if I engage in sexual intercourse, it happens when
  _____ *(I initiate it, someone else initiates it, etc.).*

- In a marriage, I believe that the wife should _____ _____ (do or act in what way?).

- In a marriage, I believe that the husband should _____ _____ (do or act in what way?).

- (If married) In my own marriage, I do _____, and my husband does _____.

- I view men as _____. (What's the first word that comes to mind?)

- I believe men are basically _____. What's more, I think men should _____.

- I believe people are powerful when they _____.

- In my own relationships, I feel powerful when I _____ _____.

- If I am feeling powerless, I may do things to try to regain power through _____.

- The most valuable thing about me is _____.

- My primary identity is as a _____.

After you complete this exercise, go back through and reread what you have written. Let the words and ideas sit with you in a quiet space. Do you like the way you are thinking, feeling and behaving in these areas? Identify some areas you can grow toward wholeness and healing in the ways you view men, women and sex. Use your journal to respond to the following sentence prompts:

- In light of who Christ is, my identity is _____.

- I am free to love _____.

- I am freed from the need to _____.

CHAPTER 4: SEXUAL SELF-IMAGE IN A GIRLS-GONE-WILD WORLD

Sexual self-image inventory. Sexual self-image includes the ways we think and feel about our bodies and about ourselves as sexual beings. Use your journal to complete this short but challenging exercise.

- Without overanalyzing or overthinking it, choose five adjectives to describe your body.

- Again, without overanalyzing or overthinking it, choose five words to describe sex (or sexual behavior).

    Read over your list. Do you notice a theme in the words you have chosen? Are they marked by fear, shame or embarrassment? If you observe a negative tone in the words you have chosen, go back and try to identify three or more positive (or at least neutral!) words to describe your body and sex.

    Finally, choose one theme word to hang on to to remind yourself of the beauty of God's creation (which includes both your body *and* sex!).

- My body is _____ *(insert a positive word, such as strong, resilient, able, nurturing, etc.).*

- Sex is (or can be) _____ *(insert a positive word that reflects the truth of God's design, such as mystery, pleasurable or a gift, etc.).*

    Remind yourself of the *truth* of these statements, even when they don't *feel* like truth. Your body and sex are good gifts. Ask God to help you grow into that truth if it feels distant and unreachable right now.

CHAPTER 5: THE SHAME OF SILENCE

Stones of shame. In this chapter several taboo topics, often covered in shame and secrecy, are discussed. You may (or may not) have felt a strong connection with one of the women described and their guilt and shame regarding their sexual feelings, thoughts or behaviors. Even if you didn't connect with the particular experiences of one of the women in this chapter, part of life in our broken world involves guilt and shame.

For this exercise you will need a few stones (small enough to carry in your pocket but large enough to feel their weight), a journal and some uninterrupted time. Begin by finding a quiet space to spend a set amount of time (ten minutes is a good start). Use that time to intentionally contemplate those things in your life that weigh you down with guilt and shame. Do not judge or evaluate, just allow the reality of those feelings to be present in you.

After the allotted period of silence and reflection, write down a single word or phrase to represent *each* of those places of shame or guilt that came to you. For example, your word list might be words or phrases such as *greed, relationship with* _____, *abortion, envy, alcohol, purging, abuse.* Write down whatever came to mind without judging or editing them.

Next, choose a stone for each word or phrase you wrote down in your journal. If you would like, you can even write that word or phrase on the stone itself. Place those stones in your pockets and carry them with you for an hour or even a day.

As you go through your day, prayerfully ask God to reveal what you are ready to let go of, release and give over to him. Some of those stones may represent unnecessary guilt that needs to be thrown away. As that becomes clear to you, find a space and time to toss away that burden. For example, if you carry guilt for abuse that was done to you, the responsibility for that shame is not yours. That burden is not yours to carry; it needs to be discarded.

You may discover that you are not yet ready to let go of some of your burdens. If so, I would encourage you to allow yourself to feel the physical weight of carrying that stone around with you for a time. Although the physical burden is small in comparison to the psychological and spiritual ones, the tangible reminder can be powerful. Ask yourself, *What keeps me from laying that particular burden of shame and silence down? How can I release the burden, at least in part, by sharing it with God and a trusted friend or counselor?*

Finally, after reflecting on and sitting with the burdens of shame you carry, prayerfully ask God to help you release them. I would encourage you to find a place to physically let go of your stones of shame. Perhaps you live close to a quiet creek or a lake. Or maybe you can go for a hike in the woods and gently lay them in the forest.

You may not feel able to do this immediately, and it is important to trust your own sense of readiness. Releasing the physical stones is not a magical cure for all future feelings of guilt or shame, but it is something tangible we can do to remind us of the truth about ourselves. When we feel burdened by shame and guilt, we can remember the weight of those stones and what it felt like to physically release them. The carrying of stones reminds us how we hold on to guilt and shame, and the physical release of the stones serves as a symbol of God's redemptive work in providing freedom from shame in Christ.

CHAPTER 6: SEX, POWER AND *FIFTY SHADES OF GREY*

Addicted to noise. In this chapter you read about the relationship between sex and power. One of the most powerful things you and I deal with on a daily basis is technology. Pornography, for example, is immediately accessible on our computers, smartphones and tablets. But it's not just pornography that is readily available. Regardless of your personal connection with pornography or sexual addiction, all addiction is about *consumption*, and we are offered a lot of choices regarding what we want to consume in our culture.

We are constantly surrounded by technological noise. Texting. Facebook. Twitter. Pinterest. Email. Voicemail. And that's just the beginning. Perhaps, in part, because of this constant noise, many of us have become addicted to a frenetic, fast-paced, always-late, never-enough-time, exhausted-and-worn-out lifestyle.

For this activity, I am going to invite you to slow down and get quiet. So often, we pray *at* God instead of (even attempting to) listen *to* God. So instead of speaking words at God in prayer, sit before God in quiet and stillness, and ask him to show you what claims your heart. It may not be sex, but perhaps other idols have taken hold of your time, energy and passion.

In an effort to avoid intimacy or escape the painful reality of your everyday life, perhaps you lose yourself in shopping or drinking or crafting or working out or planning. If addiction is about consumption, what patterns of consumption do you need to be aware of in your own life?

So just start with a small amount of time, maybe five minutes. Set a timer and then *get quiet.* Do your best to empty your mind of intrusive thoughts and to-do lists. Know that those thoughts will come, but when they do, you are free to simply let them go. Release them without chasing after them.

Silence is a discipline, so do not expect it to be easy the first time. You may notice that, when you create a silent space for yourself, it brings feelings of fear or anxiety or sadness. Sometimes stillness allows that which we are running from to catch up with us.

Although it may be frightening, only by allowing and acknowledging those painful feelings can we invite God into them. Only by taking an honest look at our own woundedness, can we truly begin the healing process. But healing takes time, and silence requires quiet, unplugging, solitude.

You'll need to resist the urge to write or journal during the exercise, so you can allow yourself to simply sit in quiet. Listening. Waiting. Resting.

After your allotted time of silence, reflect on the following questions in your journal:

- How easy or difficult was it for you to be still and quiet?

- Did you wish the amount of time was longer or shorter?

- What kinds of intrusive thoughts, feelings or images did you experience as you sat in the silence?

- How well were you able to let intrusive thoughts go versus running after them?

- What feelings were evoked in you during the time of silence?

- As you reflect on consumption in your own life, what patterns do you notice?

If you do not already consistently practice times of silence in your daily life, let me encourage you to begin carving out times of quiet. This could include five minutes of your daily prayer time, where you listen instead of speak, wait instead of ask. It could mean turning off the radio in the car when you drive to work so you can simply sit in the silence.

Our world is filled with noise at every turn, and the cost for that noise can run deep. Let external silence be a balm for your soul. You may be surprised at its healing power.

CHAPTER 7: HEALING FROM UNWANTED SEXUAL EXPERIENCES

Listen to your body. An essential element of healing is allowing yourself to feel whatever feelings accompany your story. This is easier said than done. Although you may have been taught that women are emotional and men are rational, this is a gross oversimplification. These kinds of reductionist statements deny the reality that many women (as well as men) struggle to identify or express their feelings.

When faced with painful or traumatic experiences, human beings (both males or females) do whatever we can to protect ourselves. Often, survival means numbing out or shutting down our feelings. For example, you may fear that if you allowed yourself to feel sadness about your dad's abandonment, it would open the door to a bottomless pit of depression from which you could never climb out. Or if you got in touch with anger about your unwanted sexual experience that you would become consumed with bitterness and hate.

Our fear of drowning in painful feelings sometimes leads us to ignore, stuff or medicate them. But pretending we weren't raped (for example) doesn't change the reality of the very real trauma we endured. And healing won't come without bringing both the experience and our real and valid feelings into the light.

We experience emotion in our bodies through many things, such as a quickening of the heart, a tightening of the chest or a flutter in the abdomen. These bodily sensations will give you important clues about what you are feeling, and this exercise is designed to help you use your five senses to identify feelings associated with your story.

You will need at least thirty minutes to complete this exercise. You can do this resting quietly on a couch in your living room or while taking a leisurely walk through a park. Choose whatever feels right to you—whether to stay in a solitary place or to be on the move. Regardless of the specifics of your surroundings, choose a location that is safe and peaceful.

When you are ready to begin, take five minutes to devote to each sense. For example, spend the first five minutes attending to anything you notice about what you *see*. After the five minutes of observation are up, spend a few minutes writing down your reflections. (Or, if you are walking, you can do all of your reflections at the end.) Next, spend five minutes focusing on what you *hear* (then write down your reflections), then five minutes each on *smell, taste* and *touch*. For the taste segment, you might find it helpful to use a focal point, such as by drinking a cup of tea or sucking on a mint.

At the end of your reflection time, read what you wrote about each of your senses. Sit quietly with the words and the experience you just had. Allow yourself to hear any messages your body could be telling you about feelings you need to allow yourself to feel. For example, you may have experienced (previously unnoticed) tension in your chest or neck—indicating anxiety or worry. Perhaps in the midst of focusing on one of your senses, you felt moved to tears or laughter. Attend to the emotions that this experience evoked for you.

CHAPTER 8: SEXUAL DISAPPOINTMENT

Grieve your hurts. In this chapter, disappointments that you may have experienced as a single or a married are explored. One of the most important things we can do in the face of disappointment is to name it as such. Instead of minimizing, ignoring or spiritualizing the real losses we have faced, we need to bring those places of hurt into the light. In order to grieve losses, we have to first acknowledge their presence in our hearts and minds. We cannot receive comfort or healing for loss or disappointment unless we face it directly.

You will need at least twenty minutes to complete this quieting visualization exercise, which is designed to help you listen to the hurts (and joys) in your own life. This activity is from the work of Ruth Haley Barton, a spiritual director and the author of numerous spiritual formation books, and it has helped many women I encounter at retreats or in counseling.

Use the skills you learned in the silence exercise to intentionally slow down your body and mind, and rest in the quiet. Then read the words of Barton as she guides you through a time of bringing your authentic self before God:

Sit quietly at the base of the tree that is your life and begin to notice what is true about you these days. Don't rush or try to make anything happen. Let your soul venture out and say something to you that perhaps you have had a hard time acknowledging: is there a particular joy you are celebrating? A loss you are grieving? Are there tears that have been waiting to be shed? A question that is stirring? An emotion that needs expression? . . . Don't try to do anything with what you are knowing except be with it. . . . Feel the difference between doing something with it and resting with it. Feel the difference between trying to fight it and letting God fight for you.[1]

After completing this quiet visualization, describe the "tree that is your life." Is it lush and green, sagging or lifting, strong or brittle? Write about the tree in your journal, or even depict the tree as you saw it in your mind. You could do a simple sketch, a more involved painting or even craft the tree out of clay (or Play-Doh). But remind yourself that this is not an art contest.

- What do you see when you look at this tree?

- What message is there for you in it?

- What was it like for you to sit with that tree, without trying to fix it or change it?

- What does it mean for you to let "God fight for you"?

After careful consideration of what your tree looks like *now*, imagine what your tree *could* look like, what you *want* it to look like. Prayerfully ask God to reveal to you a picture of what your tree would look like if you were able to fully experience his redemption and grace. Spend some time with that image, and then depict it as well with words or pictures.

It is essential to see both the beauty and the hurt in the tree you have right now, but it's also important to view the tree for what it is: a living, dynamic thing. No matter what you do, the tree will not stay the same. And you can be actively involved in changing and growing it into something even more beautiful! Ponder how you can join with God in growing your tree into something more fruitful.

CHAPTER 9: REDEMPTIVE SEXUALITY

Find your mission. God redeems our brokenness—not just for ourselves but also for others. In this exercise, I will encourage you to intentionally reflect on ways that God can use your own wounds as a source of healing for others. Respond to the following sentence prompts in your journal:

• Out of my own experiences with pain, I have learned _____
  _____.

• When I have been hurt, what helped most was _____
  _____.

• A time in which I experienced the love of Christ through human hands and feet was _____.

• A time when I saw God work redemptively in another person's life was _____.

• I have experienced redemption in my own life through _____
  _____.

• In my own life, a picture of redemption would be _____
  _____.

• If we are all meant to take part in God's story of redemption, I believe my part would be to _____.

If you had to summarize it in a few sentences, how would you describe what you have learned through your journey of reading this book and, hopefully, of engaging with other women?

Consider writing a statement of purpose to clarify how you want to be engaged in God's big picture of redemption. You can find an endless number of books or articles on how to write a mission statement, but the focus here is not on selling a product or following a strategy. Instead, this exercise is simply meant to help you find your place in God's kingdom work, and then "funded by the grace of God, to fill this role and to delight in it."[2]

Do this in whatever way feels natural to you, which may be by depicting this sense of calling and mission in a photograph or a song. However, here is a possible example of how to do this in writing:

> I want to participate in God's full story of redemption by using my _____ (insert your own God-given gifts and abilities, talents or roles here) to move toward emotional, spiritual and sexual healing, both personally and in the lives of my _____ (insert folks whose healing you are burdened by, such as your sister, a best friend, your husband, etc.), the women in my community and around the world. I know that I can't do this alone, and I can't do everything. But I can do something. And here is where I will start. I will _____ (insert a practical step or two that you can take right now, such as participating in a small group about sexuality, having a conversation with your sister about the messages you two received growing up, subscribing to a blog about sex trafficking, participating vocally in conversations about sexuality and womanhood in which you have remained silent before, etc.).

We know we can't do everything, but we can do something. Let's choose to allow our own wounds to be a source of compassion and healing for others. May God continue to bless you on your journey toward wholeness—both in your own life and as you serve as a beacon of light for others.

Appendix B

Growing in Community

A Group Discussion Guide

Leading a small group on a book about sexuality may feel a bit daunting, and it should! Our sexuality is intricately tied into our personhood and identity. Facilitating conversations with women about sexuality can be challenging (for many of the reasons discussed in the book!). But such discussions are also incredibly fruitful and worthwhile as we bring this part of our lives into the light of God.

Long-term feelings of fear, discomfort, embarrassment and shame can affect women's ability to openly and honestly discuss their true feelings and thoughts about sexuality in general and their experiences in particular. As you get to know the women and their stories, it is important to know when to refer to a professional. If a group member appears to be in crisis or has experienced sexual trauma without ever having processed that with a professional counselor, speak to her individually and help connect her with a local therapist.

Group guidelines. As you begin a group on this topic, let me encourage you to review several ground rules at your first meeting:

1. What is said here stays here. With a topic like sexuality, the importance of confidentiality is essential. Women need to know that, if they disclose personal experiences around sexuality, those things will not become fodder for gossip or outside-of-group con-

versations. Explicitly discuss the limits of confidentiality, such as what is allowable to say/not say to spouses. Encourage members to limit their sharing with spouses to be only their own processes, not the experiences of other group members.

2. Taboo-topic conversations are invited. Nothing is off-limits. Remind women that you want them to feel comfortable asking any questions they might have. As they read about topics like masturbation, same-sex attraction, abuse and so on, remind women that they can share or ask anything they like in this group. Follow up that invitation by modeling a safe, nonjudgmental environment for group members.

3. Remind group members to be positive and supportive in their comments to each other. Sexuality is such a loaded topic, and the last thing anyone needs is a word of judgment or criticism from another in a setting they believed to be safe. Review what a safe environment is, and encourage each member to take responsibility for making the group a safe place for each other. May your time together be full of overflowing grace and redemptive truth.

Discussion questions. These questions are designed for a group meeting in one session to discuss the whole book. However, if you would like to have more time to talk about the book with a group, these questions could be used over a number of weeks alongside the guide for going deeper in appendix A, perhaps discussing one chapter in each session.

1. Why did you choose to read this book? What were you hoping to have happen in your life as a result of reading it?

2. What is it like for you to talk about sexuality? How difficult or easy will it be for you to be honest and forthright with yourself? with the group?

3. In what ways have you witnessed the impact of the fall on sexuality in general? What ways have you experienced brokenness in your own sexuality?

4. What lessons did you learn growing up about what it means to be a girl? As a child, how would you have completed these sentences: "Girls are _____. Boys are _____."

5. Describe your response to the three models of womanhood and identity discussed in chapter 3. In what ways do you identify with the male-centered woman? the female-centered woman? the Christ-centered woman? Where do you primarily find your value and worth?

6. In what ways have you internalized cultural messages about how you should look physically or behave sexually? What practical steps can you take to respond to the negative cultural messages about women and sexuality?

7. If you could ask any anonymous question about sexuality, what would it be?

8. What do you think the appeal for so many women is of books like *Fifty Shades of Grey*?

9. How and when do you feel most powerful? Have you experienced a connection between sex and power? In what ways?

10. Even if sex *feels* dirty and wrong, the truth is that sex *is* a good and beautiful gift. What are some things you struggle to believe about sex or yourself that you know to be true in your mind, but you have trouble experiencing emotionally or in your body?

11. If you have experienced unwanted sexual contact or abuse, what is your next step in healing? (If you have not talked about your experiences with anyone and/or if they were hurtful experiences, let me encourage you again to seek out a professional counselor.)

Where are you in your healing journey, and how can you meet God and others right where you are to move forward?

12. How can you more effectively respond to the needs of the vast numbers of women who have sexually traumatic histories? If you are meeting in a group, practice listening to each other's stories — without offering advice, suggestions or even words of comfort. Just listen. Be present. Be sad and broken, and grieve for them and with them.

13. If you are single, talk about your relationship with loneliness, community and sexual behavior. If you are married, describe ways in which you have or have not experienced the three purposes of sexuality discussed (unity, fruitfulness and pleasure) in your own marriage.

14. When you hear Lisa Williams's story, how does it make you feel? In what ways can you learn from her model and respond in practical ways to needs around you?

15. Who do you most connect with in the story of the Good Samaritan? What are the blinders in your own life that keep you from really seeing the pain and needs around you? How can you begin to take off the blinders?

16. Which of the myths discussed in the book did you most relate to, and how have you observed or experienced them in your own life?

- Sex is a god or sex is evil.
- Sex equals behavior.
- Sexuality is not about gender.
- What our culture teaches about women and sexuality is true.
- Sexuality should not be talked about.
- Sex is power.

- What you have done (or had done to you) is who you are.

- You must experience erotic sexual satisfaction to be fulfilled.

- Sexuality is about the individual.

17. Reflect on the idea that sexuality is about learning to receive love. Is it easier for you to give or receive love? What could God teach you through learning to receive love from others?

18. God grows us up in Christ not only for ourselves but also for others. He has work prepared for us to do to help bring others closer to his healing and redemption. What is your next step?

Further Reading

SEXUAL ABUSE

Allender, Dan B. *The Wounded Heart: Hope for Adult Victims of Childhood Sexual Abuse.* Colorado Springs: NavPress, 1990.

Altson, Renee. *Stumbling Toward Faith.* Grand Rapids: Zondervan, 2004.

Langberg, Diane Mandt. *Counseling Survivors of Sexual Abuse.* Fairfax, VA: Xulon Press, 2003.

Maltz, Wendy. *The Sexual Healing Journey: A Guide for Survivors of Sexual Abuse.* New York: HarperPerennial, 1992.

THEOLOGY AND SEXUALITY

Anderson, Ray. *On Being Human: Essays in Theological Anthropology.* Grand Rapids: Eerdmans, 1982.

Balswick, Jack O., and Judith K. Balswick. *A Model for Marriage: Covenant, Grace, Empowerment and Intimacy.* Downers Grove, IL: IVP Academic, 2006.

Balswick, Judith K., and Jack O. Balswick. *Authentic Human Sexuality: An Integrated Christian Approach.* Downers Grove, IL: IVP Academic, 1999.

Bass, Ellen, and Laura Davis. *The Courage to Heal: A Guide for Women Survivors of Child Sexual Abuse,* 3rd edition. New York: Collins Living, 1994.

Bell, Rob. *Sex God: Exploring the Endless Connections Between Sexuality and Spirituality.* Grand Rapids: Zondervan, 2008.

Foster, Richard J. *The Challenge of the Disciplined Life: Christian Reflections on Money, Sex & Power.* San Francisco: HarperCollins, 1985.

Lewis, C. S. *The Four Loves.* New York: Harcourt Brace Jovanovich, 1960.

Smedes, Lewis B. *Sex for Christians: The Limits and Liberties of Sexual Living.* Grand Rapids: Eerdmans, 1976.

ADDICTION

Dunnington, Kent. *Addiction and Virtue: Beyond the Models of Disease and Choice*. Downers Grove, IL: IVP Academic, 2011.

Ferree, Marnie. *No Stones: Women Redeemed from Sexual Addiction*, 2nd edition. Downers Grove, IL: InterVarsity Press, 2010.

May, Gerald. *Addiction and Grace: Love and Spirituality in the Healing of Addictions*. San Francisco: HarperOne, 2007.

Schaumburg, Harry. *False Intimacy: Understanding the Struggle of Sexual Addiction*. Colorado Springs: NavPress, 1992.

Struthers, William M. *Wired for Intimacy: How Pornography Hijacks the Male Brain*. Downers Grove, IL: InterVarsity Press, 2009.

SEXUAL ORIENTATION

Hallman, Janelle. *The Heart of Female Same-Sex Attraction: A Comprehensive Counseling Resource*. Downers Grove, IL: InterVarsity Press, 2008.

Hill, Wesley. *Washed and Waiting: Reflections on Christian Faithfulness and Homosexuality*. Grand Rapids: Zondervan, 2010.

Lee, Justin. *Torn: Rescuing the Gospel from the Gays-Vs.-Christians Debate*. New York: Jericho Books, 2013.

Marin, Andrew. *Love Is an Orientation: Elevating the Conversation with the Gay Community*. Downers Grove, IL: InterVarsity Press, 2009.

Paris, Jenell Williams. *The End of Sexual Identity: Why Sex Is Too Important to Define Who We Are*. Downers Grove, IL: InterVarsity Press, 2011.

Yuan, Christopher, and Angela Yuan. *Out of a Far Country: A Gay Son's Journey to God; A Broken Mother's Search for Hope*. Colorado Springs: WaterBrook, 2011.

SEXUAL FUNCTIONING

Hart, Archibald D., Catherine Hart Weber and Debra L. Taylor. *Secrets of Eve: Understanding Female Sexuality*. Nashville: Word Publishing, 1998.

Penner, Clifford, and Joyce Penner. *The Gift of Sex: A Guide to Sexual Fulfillment*. Nashville: W Publishing, 2003.

Rosenau, Douglas. *A Celebration of Sex: A Guide to Enjoying God's Gift of Married Sexual Pleasure*. Nashville: Thomas Nelson, 1994.

Schnarch, David. *Passionate Marriage: Keeping Love & Intimacy Alive in Committed Relationships*. New York: Owl Books, 1997.

SINGLENESS AND SEXUALITY

Peterson, Margaret Kim, and Dwight N. Peterson. *Are You Waiting for "The One"? Cultivating Realistic, Positive Expectations for Christian Marriage*. Downers Grove, IL: InterVarsity Press, 2011.

Rosenau, Douglas, and Michael Todd Wilson. *Soul Virgins: Redefining Single Sexuality*. Grand Rapids: Baker, 2006.

WOMEN, CULTURE AND SEXUALITY

Levy, Ariel. *Female Chauvinist Pigs: Women and the Rise of Raunch Culture*. New York: Free Press, 2005.

McMinn, Lisa. *Sexuality and Holy Longing: Embracing Intimacy in a Broken World*. San Francisco: Jossey-Bass, 2004.

Meeker, Margaret. *Strong Fathers, Strong Daughters: 10 Secrets Every Father Should Know*. New York: Ballantine, 2007.

Winner, Lauren. *Real Sex: The Naked Truth About Chastity*. Grand Rapids: Brazos, 2005.

Acknowledgments

Gary Deddo suggested I write this book several years ago, and I am deeply grateful for his encouragement, patience and theological insight. I am honored to be part of InterVarsity Press, a publisher whose books I am challenged by and proudly suggest to clients and friends, students and colleagues. A special thanks to Cindy Bunch, who helped me focus the book on practicality and real women. It is a gift to be supported by a team of smart women at IVP: Lorraine Caulton, Adrianna Wright, Alisse Wissman and Elaina Whittenhall.

I taught an undergraduate seminar on the psychology of women for several years at Lee University, and my students' contributions to discussions about the media and entertainment industry are reflected in chapter 4. Teaching that class has been one of the great joys of my career, and I am blessed to call many of those students friends today.

Many other friends and colleagues provided clinical and editorial feedback, and the book is stronger for it. I am grateful to Jacquelyn Delgado, Kate Gilliard, Farron Kilburn, Jennette Leal, Charity Lusk-Muse, Kauri Tallant and Meaghan Warnock for their contributions. A special thank you to Dr. Amanda Blackburn; both the book and my life are richer for our friendship.

In my work I have been privileged to sit with women struggling with questions about identity, gender, relationships and sexuality.

Many pieces of their stories are reflected in these pages, with identifying details and information changed in order to protect their privacy. For each of you who have trusted me to be part of your journey, thank you. I have thought and prayed and fought for you in all the ways I know to do, and I truly believe that your stories can be a light for others.

Tom and Sue Gaines took their grandparent duties very seriously to help me finish this book. In their fifty years of marriage, they have modeled love, friendship and commitment, and my own marriage and family is stronger for it. My mom read every word and strengthened the book's scope with her questions and curiosity.

My husband, Jeff, has been a staunch believer in the need for this book and in my ability to write it; his compassion and insight is woven throughout, especially in chapters 5 and 6. Completing this project took many years, perhaps because we kept adding babies and noise to our home. These "distractions" have enlarged our lives and hearts: Tommy, Brennan, Lily and Oliver—I am proud and lucky to be your mom.

And above all, I am thankful for a God who redeems and restores us in every way. Who we are is not what we have done or had done to us; rather who we are is who we are becoming in Christ—that is a gift indeed.

Notes

CHAPTER 1: YOU ARE SEXUAL AND IT IS GOOD

[1]Philip Yancey, *Rumors of Another World: What on Earth Are We Missing?* (Grand Rapids: Zondervan, 2003), pp. 78-79.

[2]See James Torrance, *Worship, Community & the Triune God of Grace* (Downers Grove, IL: InterVarsity Press, 1996), p. 104.

CHAPTER 2: MORE THAN AN ACT

[1]Ariel Levy, *Female Chauvinist Pigs: Women and the Rise of Raunch Culture* (New York: Free Press, 2005), p. 31.

[2]Associated Press, "Anthony Weiner Resigns: Timeline of Photos, Twitter Scandal Fallout," *Huffington Post*, June 16, 2011, http://huffingtonpost .com/2011/06/16/anthony-weiner-resigns-scandal_n_878161.html.

[3]For further reading on the nature of the Trinity, see Ray Anderson, *On Being Human: Essays in Theological Anthropology* (Grand Rapids: Eerdmans, 1982); or Gary Deddo, "Why We're Gendered Beings—A Trinitarian Perspective: The Difference Difference Makes" (Evangelical Theological Society, November 2006), www.trinitystudycenter.com/topical/trinityand gender.pdf.

[4]This is typically accompanied by the complementary anatomy and subsequent development of secondary sex characteristics and hormones. For intersex individuals, however, this is not the case.

[5]Merriam-Webster's online dictionary, s.v. "sex," www.m-w.com/dictionary/sex. "Sexual intercourse" is then further defined as "1: heterosexual intercourse involving penetration of the vagina by the penis; 2: intercourse (anal or oral intercourse) that does not involve penetration of the vagina by the penis." Retrieved at the Merriam-Webster's online dictionary at www.m-w.com /dictionary/sexual+intercourse.

[6]Lewis Smedes, *Sex for Christians* (Grand Rapids: Eerdmans, 1994), p. 16.

[7]C. S. Lewis, *The Four Loves* (New York: Harcourt Brace Jovanovich, 1960), p. 139.

[8]Lisa Sowle Cahill, *Sex, Gender & Christian Ethics* (Cambridge: Cam-

bridge University Press, 1996), p. 111.

[9]Lewis, *Four Loves*, p. 91.

CHAPTER 3: BEYOND THE BATTLE OF THE SEXES

[1]See suggestions for further reading for books that address men and masculinity.

[2]Linda Hirshman, "Is Your Husband a Worse Problem Than Larry Summers?" *Inside Higher Ed*, December 9, 2005, www.insidehighered.com/views/2005/12/09/hirshman#ixzz1diaBPGPT.

[3]*Lean In* (New York: Alfred A. Knopf, 2013), p. 24.

[4]Gordon D. Fee, "Male and Female in the New Creation," in Ronald W. Pierce and Rebecca Merrill Groothuis, eds., *Discovering Biblical Equality: Complementarity Without Hierarchy*, 2nd ed. (Downers Grove, IL: InterVarsity Press, 2005), p. 177, emphasis added.

[5]Judith K. Balswick and Jack O. Balswick, "Marriage as a Partnership of Equals" in *Discovering Biblical Equality: Complementarity Without Hierarchy*, 2nd ed., ed. Ronald W. Pierce and Rebecca Merrill Groothuis, (Downers Grove, IL: InterVarsity Press, 2005), p. 460.

CHAPTER 4: SEXUAL SELF-IMAGE IN A GIRLS-GONE-WILD WORLD

[1]The Schapiro Group, "Men Who Buy Sex with Adolescent Girls: A Scientific Research Study" (Atlanta: Schapiro Group, 2010), www.womensfundingnetwork.org/sites/wfnet.org/files/AFNAP/TheSchapiroGroupGeorgiaDemandStudy.pdf.

[2]As quoted in Ariel Levy, *Female Chauvinist Pigs: Women and the Rise of Raunch Culture* (New York: Free Press, 2005), p. 19.

[3]As quoted in Lauren Winner, *Real Sex: The Naked Truth About Chasity* (Grand Rapids: Brazos, 2005), p. 18.

[4]Usher, featuring Ludacris and Lil Jon, "Yeah!" *Confessions* (Nashville: Arista Records, 2004). Written by Lil Jon, Sean Garrett, Patrick J. Que Smith, Ludacris, Robert McDowell and LRoc.

[5]C. L. Muehlenhard and M. A. Linton, "Date Rape and Sexual Aggression in Dating Situations," *Journal of Counseling Psychology* 34 (1987): 186-96.

[6]C. Neal and M. Mangis, "Unwanted Sexual Experiences Among Christian College Women: Saying No on the Inside," *Journal of Psychology and Theology* 23, no. 3 (1995): 171-79.

[7]M. P. Koss, C. A. Gidycz and N. Wisniewski, "The Scope of Rape," *Journal of Consulting and Clinical Psychology* 55 (1987): 162-70.

CHAPTER 5: THE SHAME OF SILENCE

[1]"Surveillence Summary," *Morbidity Mortality Weekly Review* 53 (May 21, 2004): 17, as quoted in Margaret Meeker, *Strong Fathers, Strong Daughters: 10 Secrets Every Father Should Know* (New York: Ballantine, 2007), p. 20.

[2]Lisa Graham McMinn, *Sexuality and Holy Longing: Embracing Intimacy in a Broken World* (San Francisco: Jossey-Bass, 2004), p. 61.

[3]Lauren Winner, *Real Sex: The Naked Truth About Chastity* (Grand Rapids: Brazos, 2005), p. 121.

[4]McMinn, *Sexuality and Holy Longing*, p. 53.

[5]Jenell Williams Paris, *The End of Sexual Identity: Why Sex Is Too Important to Define Who We Are* (Downers Grove, IL: IVP Books, 2011), p. 27.

[6]Philip Yancey, *What's So Amazing About Grace?* (Grand Rapids: Zondervan, 1997), p. 152.

[7]Paris, *End of Sexual Identity*, p. 22.

CHAPTER 6: SEX, POWER AND *FIFTY SHADES OF GREY*

[1]As quoted in *The New York Times* (October 28, 1973).

[2]E. L. James, *Fifty Shades of Grey* (New York: Vintage Books, 2011), p. 117.

[3]Tim Alan Gardner, *Sacred Sex: A Spiritual Celebration of Oneness in Marriage* (Colorado Springs: WaterBrook, 2002), p. 105.

[4]Kent Dunnington, *Addiction and Virtue: Beyond the Models of Disease and Choice* (Downers Grove, IL: IVP Academic, 2011), p. 151.

[5]Betty Friedan, *The Feminine Mystique* (New York: Dell, 1963), p. 267.

[6]William Struthers, *Wired for Intimacy: How Pornography Hijacks the Male Brain* (Downers Grove, IL: InterVarsity Press, 2009), p. 99.

[7]Rob Bell, *Sex God: Exploring the Endless Connections Between Sexuality and Spirituality* (Grand Rapids: Zondervan, 2007), p. 77.

[8]Jack O. Balswick and Judith K. Balswick, *A Model for Marriage: Covenant, Grace, Empowerment and Intimacy* (Downers Grove, IL: InterVarsity Press, 2006), p. 69.

[9]James Bryan Smith, *The Good and Beautiful God* (Downers Grove, IL: IVP Books, 2009), p. 161.

CHAPTER 7: HEALING FROM UNWANTED SEXUAL EXPERIENCES

[1]There are many excellent books on healing from sexual abuse, including Wendy Maltz, *The Sexual Healing Journey: A Guide for Survivors of Sexual Abuse*, 3rd ed. (New York: William Morrow, 2012); and Ellen Bass and

Laura Davis, *The Courage to Heal: A Guide for Women Survivors of Child Sexual Abuse*, 4th ed. (New York: HarperCollins, 2008).

[2]C. Courtois, *Healing the Incest Wound: Adult Survivors in Therapy* (New York: Norton, 1988), p. 16.

[3]The Federal Child Abuse Prevention and Treatment Act defines sexual abuse as: "the employment, use, persuasion, inducement, enticement, or coercion of any child to engage in, or assist any other person to engage in, any sexually explicit conduct or simulation of such conduct for the purpose of producing a visual depiction of such conduct; or the rape, and in cases of caretaker or inter-familial relationships, statutory rape, molestation, prostitution, or other forms of sexual exploitation of children, or incest with children," taken from Child Welfare Information Gateway, "What Is Child Abuse and Neglect?" *Factsheets*, 2008, www.childwelfare.gov/pubs/factsheets/whatiscan.cfm. See also the Stop It Now! page for what is considered child sexual abuse: www.stopitnow.org/warning_signs_csa_definition; or see HealthyChildren.org for information on safety and prevention of sexual abuse: www.healthychildren.org/English/safety-prevention/at-home/Pages/Sexual-Abuse.aspx.

[4]Child Welfare Information Gateway, "Child Sexual Abuse: Intervention and Treatment Issues" (McLean, VA: The Circle, 1993), www.childwelfare.gov/pubs/usermanuals/sexabuse.

[5]Margaret J. Blythe, J. Dennis Fortenberry, M'Hamed Temkit, Wanzhu Tu and Donald P. Orr, "Incidence and Correlates of Unwanted Sex in Relationships of Middle and Late Adolescent Women," *Archives of Pediatric & Adolescent Medicine* 160, no. 206 (2006): 591-95, referenced in Margaret Meeker, *Strong Fathers, Strong Daughters: 10 Secrets Every Father Should Know* (New York: Ballantine Books, 2007), p. 20.

[6]C. L. Muehlenhard and M. A. Linton, "Date Rape and Sexual Aggression in Dating Situations," *Journal of Counseling Psychology* 34 (1987): 186-96. C. Neal and M. Mangis, "Unwanted Sexual Experiences Among Christian College Women: Saying No on the Inside," *Journal of Psychology and Theology* 23, no. 3 (1995): 171-79. M. P. Koss, C. A. Gidycz and N. Wisniewski, "The Scope of Rape," *Journal of Consulting and Clinical Psychology* 55 (April 1987): 162-70.

[7]Lisa Graham McMinn, *Sexuality and Holy Longing: Embracing Intimacy in a Broken World* (San Francisco: Jossey-Bass, 2004), p. 45.

[8]Wendy Maltz, *The Sexual Healing Journey* (New York: HarperPerennial, 1991), p. 4.

9Diane Langberg, *Counseling Survivors of Sexual Abuse* (Fairfax, VA: Xulon Press, 2003) p. 142.

10Maltz, *Sexual Healing Journey*, p. 45.

11Lauren Winner, *Real Sex: The Naked Truth About Chastity* (Grand Rapids: Brazos, 2005), p. 109.

12Douglas Rosenau, *A Celebration of Sex: A Guide to Enjoying God's Gift of Married Sexual Pleasure* (Nashville: Thomas Nelson, 1994), p. 319.

13Maltz, *Sexual Healing Journey*, p. 91.

14See Langberg, *Counseling Survivors*, p. 142.

CHAPTER 8: SEXUAL DISAPPOINTMENT

1Statistics retrieved from Linda Petty, "Single? You're Not Alone," *CNN Living* (August 20, 2010), http://articles.cnn.com/2010-08-19/living/single .in.america_1_single-fathers-single-mothers-single-parents?_s= PM:LIVING.

2Sabrina Tavernise, "Married Couples Are No Longer a Majority, Census Finds," *The New York Times* (May 26, 2011), www.nytimes.com/2011/05/26 /us/26marry.html.

3M. Gay Hubbard, *Women: The Misunderstood Majority* (Dallas: Word, 1992), p. 138.

4A. D. Hart, C. H. Weber, and D. L. Taylor, *Secrets of Eve: Understanding the Mystery of Female Sexuality* (Nashville: Word, 1998) p. 220.

5M. K. Peterson and D. N. Peterson, *Are You Waiting for "The One"? Cultivating Realistic, Positive Expectations for Christian Marriage* (Downers Grove, IL: IVP Books, 2011), p. 150.

6Clifford and Joyce Penner, *The Gift of Sex: A Guide to Sexual Fulfillment* (Nashville: W Publishing, 2003), p. 48.

7Two excellent books are the Penners' *Gift of Sex*; and Douglas E. Rosenau's *A Celebration of Sex* (Nashville: Thomas Nelson, 1994).

8Lewis Smedes, *Sex for Christians: The Limits and Liberties of Sexual Living* (Grand Rapids: Eerdmans, 1976), p. 33.

CHAPTER 9: REDEMPTIVE SEXUALITY

1Jacque Wilson, "Prostituted Children Find Refuge," *CNN* online, August 31, 2011, www.cnn.com/2011/US/08/31/lisa.williams.living.water.girls/index .html.

2Ibid.

3Ibid.

4I am grateful to Pastor David Sternberg for his insights on this passage in a sermon given at Bridge Christian Church on August 26, 2012.

5Gabe Lyons, *unChristian: What a New Generation Really Thinks About Christianity . . . and Why It Matters* (Grand Rapids: Baker Books, 2007), p. 27.

6Bob Goff, *Love Does* (Nashville: Thomas Nelson, 2012), p. 201.

7Cornelius Plantinga Jr., *Not the Way It's Supposed to Be: A Breviary of Sin* (Grand Rapids: Eerdmans, 1995), p. 197.

APPENDIX B: GOING DEEPER: A STUDY GUIDE FOR INDIVIDUAL GROWTH AND REFLECTION

1Ruth Haley Barton, *Sacred Rhythms: Arranging Our Lives for Spiritual Transformation* (Downers Grove, IL: IVP Books, 2006), pp. 43-44.

2Cornelius Plantinga Jr., *Not the Way It's Supposed to Be: A Breviary of Sin* (Grand Rapids: Eerdmans, 1995), p. 197.

Some voices challenge us. Others support or encourage us. Voices can move us to change our minds, draw close to God, discover a new spiritual gift. The voices of others are shaping who we are.

The voices behind IVP Crescendo join together to draw us into God's story. We'll discover God's work around the globe even as we learn to love the people around the corner. We'll have opportunity to heal our places of pain. We'll discover new ways to love our families. We'll hear God's voice speaking into our lives as we discover new places of influence.

IVP Crescendo invites you to join in the rising chorus

- *to listen to the voices of others*
- *to hear the voice of God*
- *and to grow your own voice in*

COURAGE. CONFIDENCE. CALLING.

---

ivpress.com/crescendo
ivpress.com/crescendo-social

Also by Kim Gaines Eckert

Stronger than You Think:
Becoming Whole Without Having to Be Perfect.
A Woman's Guide

978-0-8308-3373-3